YESTERDAY'S YORKSHIRE

FOLLOWING PAGE
Halifax from Beacon Hill, 1967.
The stone sets used for the background were photographed near the North Bridge area of the town.

YESTERDAY'S YORKSHIRE

A Celebration of the Industrial West Riding

TERRY SUTTON

THE DOVECOTE PRESS

For Susan

Kitchen tiles, Crackenedge, Dewsbury.

First published in 2001 by The Dovecote Press Ltd
Stanbridge, Wimborne, Dorset BH21 4JD

ISBN 1 874336 89 X

© Terry Sutton 2001

Terry Sutton has asserted his rights under the Copyright, Designs
and Patent Act 1988 to be identified as author of this work

Designed by The Dovecote Press

Typeset in Monotype Sabon

Printed and bound by KHL Printing, Singapore

A CIP catalogue record for this book is available
from the British Library

CONTENTS

ACKNOWLEDGEMENTS

What started out in the 1960s as a single-handed journey with a sketch book and camera round the Industrial West Riding became very much a shared experience. My grateful thanks to Tony Mellor for his influence in the early years of my career in advertising and for his help in staging my first exhibition at the School of Art & Design, Batley, in 1976. To all my friends at the School of Art & Design, the Northern Centre for Digital Imaging, Batley, and the University of Huddersfield for their encouragement and support during the evolution of this book, with special thanks to Julie Hilditch, Warren Sykes, Mike Oliver and Ian Ingram. To John Holroyd for what seems like a lifetime of mutual interest in all things ordinary and extraordinary about the area in which we live, and for contributing to the book from his extensive photo archive; pages 106 (middle) and 109.

My search for archive pictures has been greatly rewarded and the contents of the book enhanced by the work of David Holmes, page 107; Peter Sunderland, page 114; Woods Visual Imaging, pages 33 (top) and 82; The Leslie Overend Collection (Courtesy of the National Railway Museum), page 111; Porl Medlock, pages 78 (right) and 79; Fred Hartley (Courtesy of Kirklees Digital Archive Community History Service), pages 28 and 58; Huddersfield Daily Examiner (Courtesy of Kirklees Digital Archive Community History Service), pages 60 and 83; The Alice Longstaff Gallery Collection (Courtesy of Frank Woolrych), page 140.

I am also indebted to the following for searching their picture archives: The Bradford Industrial Museum, pages 12, 18, 23, 31 (bottom right), 73 (right) and 142 (right); Calderdale Industrial Museum, page 96 (bottom right); Joshua Tetley & Son (Courtesy of West Yorkshire Archive Service, Leeds), page 98 (left); Yorkshire Co-operatives Ltd. (Courtesy of West Yorkshire Archive Service, Bradford, page 66 (bottom left); Bond Publications, page 102.

Stephen Chapman of Bellcode Books, Norman Ellis, and Michael Park, Hon. Secretary The Yorkshire Dialect Society also responded kindly to my requests for information, as did the library staff at; Calderdale Libraries; Halifax and Sowerby Bridge, Kirklees Libraries; Huddersfield, Cleckheaton and Heckmondwike. Bradford Central Library, Wakefield Library. The staff of Copy Concept, Cleckheaton, have also been supportive.

The task would have been well nigh impossible without the patience and tolerance of my family, who once again endured my lengthy take-over bid for our PC and dining room table.

And finally, my sincere thanks to my publisher David Burnett for his guidance and enthusiasm in enabling me to turn a notion and a few 'thumbnails' into reality.

TERRY SUTTON
Cleckheaton
OCTOBER 2001

INTRODUCTION

I can just remember the street party to celebrate the end of the Second World War, although the full significance of the occasion would have been lost on a four-year-old at the time. The air-raid shelter in the middle of Greenroyd Avenue, Hunsworth, on the outskirts of Cleckheaton, which thankfully never had to shield its residents from anything approaching even a near miss, would soon be demolished. Gas masks and black-out material would be consigned to the loft or garden shed, although rationing would rule our lives for a few more years, reminding us that the road to recovery would be a long one.

Leeds and Bradford had become targets for the Luftwaffe, but mercifully the destruction there was nothing like that suffered by Sheffield and Hull. The war was over, and as the mills and factories returned to peacetime production, the towns of the West Riding were much as their Victorian architects and builders had created them.

Home life in the first decade after the war was very different to today. BBC radio seemed to be mostly for grown-ups, and without the distractions of computers, television and video, children like myself had 'hobbies'. The dining table in the front room of our house would, at one end, be covered in bits of Meccano; God's gift to budding engineers like my brother Leslie, who had a natural flair for creating working model cranes, tractors, railway engines and other mechanical marvels. At the other end of the table were pencils, paints, crayons and myself, filling yet another drawing book with pictures of trains, aircraft, tanks and ships – and yet more trains.

The pattern of our future working lives was set there and then. Leslie became an engineer and I joined the 'great unwashed' by becoming an art student at the School of Art & Design, Batley. In the years before vocational courses brought a breath of reality to art and design education, art traditions going back centuries were still strong at Batley. The smell of oil paints and turpentine filled the air. Canvas, cartridge paper, gouache and clay were our raw materials. It is important that artists react to their surroundings. To this end, our tutors would send us out into the streets and alleyways of Batley or a bus ride beyond, spiral bound sketchbooks and 2B pencils in hand, to grapple with perspective and freehand drawing.

Until the early 1960s Batley was the archetypal Yorkshire mill town. Its mills, warehouses, rows of stone terraced houses, corner shops, fish and chip shops and pubs could have provided the backdrop to any one of the 'kitchen sink' dramas beloved of playwrights and film makers at the time.

Towards the end of my student days, the wind of change began to blow through the industrial West Riding in the shape of Clean Air Acts, smokeless zones and slum clearance. This meant the end of the road for the terraced housing behind the School of Art. The demolition teams worked their way through Hume Street, Providence Street, Cobden Street and the incongruously named Bright Street; a world of gas lighting, stone sinks and outside toilets. Although their demise came not a moment too soon, the clearing dust from each crash of masonry and timber often revealed a cast iron fireplace, a row of decorative sink corner tiles, or a pre-war wallpaper pattern on what was once a bedroom wall. Such scenes were then commonplace, and were being duplicated throughout the West Riding on an almost daily basis.

My metamorphosis from art student to commercial artist in a Leeds advertising agency meant that my new found 'wealth' enabled me to buy a 35mm single lens reflex camera – maybe not as analytical as a sketchbook, but much more immediate! The fascination for places and things on my own doorstep was rekindled. Armed with my new camera I began photographing the last remnants of the world into which I had been born, and which was now being so energetically destroyed. By the mid-1970s I had taken over two thousand photographs. From these a number of illustrations in gouache and coloured inks were done and in 1976 I had my first exhibition at the School of Art

Holbeck, Leeds, November 1961, from an art school sketchbook showing high-rise housing rising from the rubble of back-to-back terraces.

& Design, Batley. Shortly after this I became a full-time lecturer in graphic design and, after a further exhibition at the Bradford Industrial Museum the negatives, photographs and illustrations were consigned to the loft, where they lay undisturbed for over twenty years. Attics and lofts are built to store and later, sometimes much later, to rummage for things. And so it was, at the approach to a new millennium that I rediscovered part of my past and realised that the world in which I now lived had changed dramatically. My enthusiasm for the everyday scenes of yesteryear was once again revived, and an illustration of a rusting quarry steam crane became the first of a new set painted especially for this book

The 1960s and 1970s were a time of great change, especially for the young. The Beatles and their contemporaries, 'flower-power', political satirists, high-rise housing, and the advent of the 'pill' were all part of a more liberal thinking Britain. The smoky haze of my own largely Victorian influenced childhood was to be gradually, if never fully, dispersed. The increase in car ownership brought with it another kind of liberation, making us, if not more independent, less community minded. In the years before the word 'lifestyle' came into our vocabulary, styles of living were definitely changing.

Between 1953 and 1973, my home town of Cleckheaton said goodbye to two cinemas, two railway stations, chapels - one the size of a small cathedral, lock-up shops, mills and a maltings.

Many of these buildings were left to the mercies of the elements before the coup de grâce was applied; as though we might have second thoughts before consigning them to eternity. Deserted terraced houses, mills and chapels, dilapidated wool warehouses, cinemas, railway stations and goods yards, with their crumbling stone and brickwork, provided a wealth of colours and textures.

During one of my Sunday morning excursions into the nooks and crannies of the industrial West Riding I came across the half demolished remains of an optician's lock-up shop in Dewsbury. There on a spike, amongst the rubble, was a sheaf of letterheads, some beautifully engraved in copperplate script, dating back to 1908, with correspondence relating to the repair of a clock for the Mirfield Gas Company; an order for a bicycle from the Crescent Cycle Company, Birmingham – 'we are despatching your machine tonight, and hope that it will reach you safely and be entirely to your satisfaction'; and a brief black edged note telling of the death of a relative in the Dewsbury workhouse. Here, to bring my fanciful ideas in photography and illustration down to earth, was a reminder that the passing of these ordinary things amounted to much more than just bricks and mortar.

The years between slum clearance and supermarkets were a kind of backwater, when, without realising it, we were saying goodbye to the last vestiges of the 'machine age' and the way of life that went with it. Pocket calculators, microwave ovens and digital watches heralded the new era of 'must have' technology.

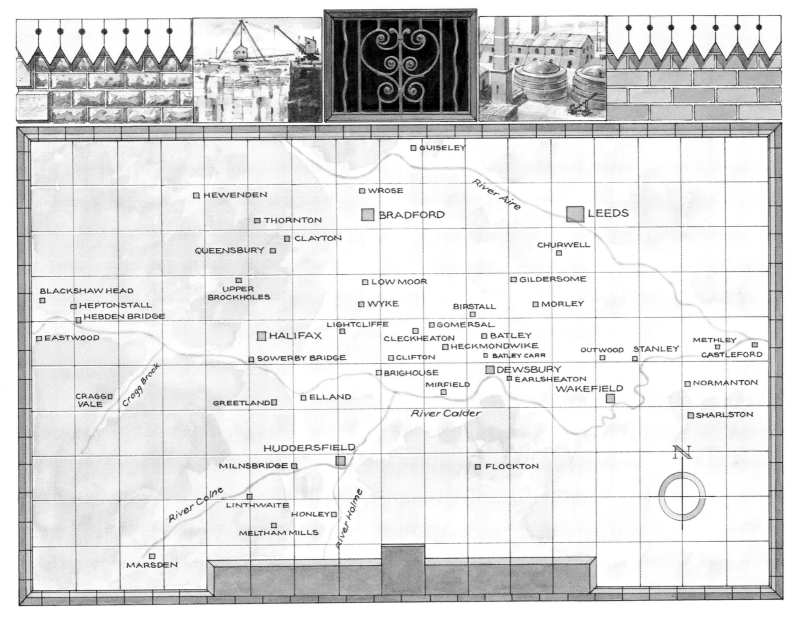

Increasing car ownership meant that shopping has joined sport in our increasingly leisure orientated world where, paradoxically, the word 'heritage' is now highly visible in tourist information centres. Pedestrian precincts with their cobblestones, iron bollards and other neo-Victorian street furniture are now a feature of our town centres. Mills have become industrial museums, and the sight and sound of a steam train in action can still be found on some Yorkshire branch lines.

We cannot hope to find a place for everything from the past. Inevitably, history has to be polished and packaged to take its place in our ever changing present. Our appreciation of it amounts to much more than mere sentiment or nostalgia; it is the foundation of every aspect of our lives.

The Boggart Stone, on Widdop Moor, high above the Calder Valley.

MILLSTONE
GRIT

Above one of the windows of a wool warehouse in Dewsbury there is the carved head of a young Queen Victoria. This hidden masterpiece, the work of a long forgotten journeyman stonemason, was sculpted from sandstone formed 300 million years ago on the rain-washed moors that form the backdrop to the industrial landscape of West Yorkshire.

Quarrying in the Pennines can be traced back to medieval times, when stone roofing slates or 'thakstones' and millstones for grinding corn were quarried. Records show that two millstones were brought from Grindlestone bank in Ovenden Wood for Halifax Mill, presumably for grinding and sharpening wool cropper's shears.

Farming was then the predominant occupation, but by the reign of Elizabeth I the fledgling textile industry had begun to

BELOW 'This hidden masterpiece'. A wool warehouse in Dewsbury displays a local stonemason's contribution to the richness of our industrial past in a carved head of the young Queen Victoria.
BELOW RIGHT The foundation stone of Cleckheaton Town Hall. William Anderton, his brother James and their father George were actively involved in local affairs throughout the Spen Valley.

make a significant impression on the local economy. Prosperous wool merchants and yeoman clothiers invested their wealth in fine houses with mullioned windows built of local stone, many of which still survive and are now regarded as some of the most important domestic buildings in West Yorkshire.

The mechanisation of the textile and other industries and the growth of the towns increased the demand for stone. Quarrying became a major industry in some areas, particularly around Halifax and Bradford, and where by the middle of the nineteenth century there were literally hundreds of quarries.

Quarrying employed a number of skilled crafts, and like other industries had its own vocabulary. Delvers for example, cut the stone out of the quarry face with picks, wedges and crowbars. To split stone, wooden wedges were driven into a crack and thoroughly doused with water, causing the wood to expand and the layers of the stone to split open.

Large rocks were also split using a line of 'plug and feathers', metal flanges and wedges that widened under the blows of a hammer – a process still in use today. In the nineteenth century steam cranes were used to lift large blocks of stone, whilst mechanical sawing and planing machinery was gradually introduced. Masons shaped and dressed the stone with chisel and mallet, often using a variety of decorative tooled surfaces.

Stone was 'exported' to other parts of the country by canal and railway. The original London Bridge of 1831, now a tourist attraction in the United States, used Southowram stone, which also paved some of the capital's streets.

The Pennines can be a harsh and isolated place, especially in winter. Sometimes men were 'frozen off the job' for days, which meant no pay. But quarrymen and their families were a hardy breed, and it was they who gave industry and commerce it's mills, banks, town halls and railway stations, and to whom the ordinary working family was indebted for their house, corner shop, library, public house and place of worship.

Quarrymen using a line of 'plug and feathers' to split stone at a Lightcliffe quarry.

Piercing the skyline above Halifax and the Calder Valley stands a 253 foot high tower. Built by John Edward Wainhouse, it was originally intended as a chimney for his Washer Lane Dye Works. Although no longer required as a chimney due to the sale of the dye works during its construction, Wainhouse was determined to finish the project and appointed Richard Swarbrick Dugdale to oversee its completion and design its extraordinary summit, which can be reached by climbing 403 steps.

Intricate carvings of animals and flowers adorn shoddy selling houses
in Station Road, Batley.

A long abandoned steam crane on the moors above Greetland near Halifax.

BRICK
BY BRICK

On the edge of the moors above Bradford stands Julius Whitehead's magnificent chimney. Once part of a flourishing clay pipe and fireclay works, this lone sentinel brought the colourful visual language of brick to the very heartland of stone.

The words Pennine town immediately evoke images of stone terraced houses, mills and cobbled streets. An idealised vision, and largely true of places like Hebden Bridge, Halifax, Bradford, and Huddersfield, where nearby quarries provided the basic building materials. However, take a train journey from Hebden Bridge in the Pennine foothills, to Wakefield, where the land levels out eastwards towards the Vale of York, and in a

LEFT A selection of locally made bricks.
RIGHT A monument to the hundreds of West Riding brick makers. Now a listed building, Julius Whitehead's magnificent chimney is all that remains of a once flourishing clay pipe and fireclay works at Clayton on the outskirts of Bradford.
BELOW The embossed name on a glazed tile from Julius Whitehead's Clayton works.

distance of thirty miles or so Victorian architects and builders, by using brick, changed the outlook and character of the urban landscape.

The reason for this transformation had more to do with economics than aesthetics, brick clays being usually found wherever there are coal measures. Many collieries and ironworks throughout the West Riding produced their own bricks from the fireclay just below the coal seams. By the mid-nineteenth century there were scores of brickworks in the area, literally turning out bricks by the billion.

Until the nineteenth century when machinery was gradually introduced, brickmaking was done by hand in small brickyards. In this respect there was an affinity between brickmakers and potters. David Dunderdale & Co. was a combined pottery and brickworks at Whitwood Mere near Castleford.

After digging the clay in the autumn, it was left to weather until spring when it was ground and processed in a horse-operated pugmill, a large iron or wooden tub with a central rotating shaft with projecting blades that sliced and kneaded the clay.

The brickmaker at his bench would work the clay by hand to

form a clot, before throwing it with sufficient force and skill to fill every corner of the wooden brick mould. After trimming the excess clay from the top with a wire bow, the brick would be turned out onto a pallet to be placed on a hack or drying platform. In pallet moulding the bench and mould were first dusted with sand. Many brickmakers in the West Riding used the slop moulding technique whereby the brickmaker wets the mould instead of sanding it. In both methods the brick would then be left to dry before being fired.

Because brickmaking was a regional craft, different types of kiln were used throughout the country. Three types were in general use in the West Riding. Circular downdraught kilns, similar in shape to a beehive, where the heat rose up to the dome-shaped roof to be drawn down through the stack of bricks and out via a flue at the base leading to an external chimney. In an updraught kiln, the hot fire gasses were drawn from the base of the kiln through the stack by a chimney above. In both methods, anything from a hundred to a hundred thousand bricks were stacked and fired in one operation. After firing and cooling, the bricks were removed and the operation repeated.

The Hoffmann kiln, patented in 1858 and named after its inventor, used a series of chambers. Each chamber was loaded, fired, cooled and emptied in sequence and the waste heat was used to preheat the succeeding set of bricks. In 1862 the first 'Hoffmann' type of kiln in England was ordered by John Craven for his brickworks at Roundwood near Wakefield.

Hard, anonymous, and uncompromisingly geometric, each individual brick is bonded to its neighbours to form a material framework to our domestic and working lives. Only through decay or demolition are bricks likely to reveal their identity and individuality.

In the rubble that represents the transition between past and future, bricks stand out like tombstones in a graveyard of past brickmakers and brickworks, with their names, or more intriguingly initials, imprinted in the frog or recess in the top of each brick: WHITAKER LEEDS, FENAY BRIDGE, BOWLING IRON

Like hundreds of brick and fireclay works in the West Riding, Wrose, near Bradford, has disappeared without trace. Note the circular beehive kilns in this 1934 photograph.

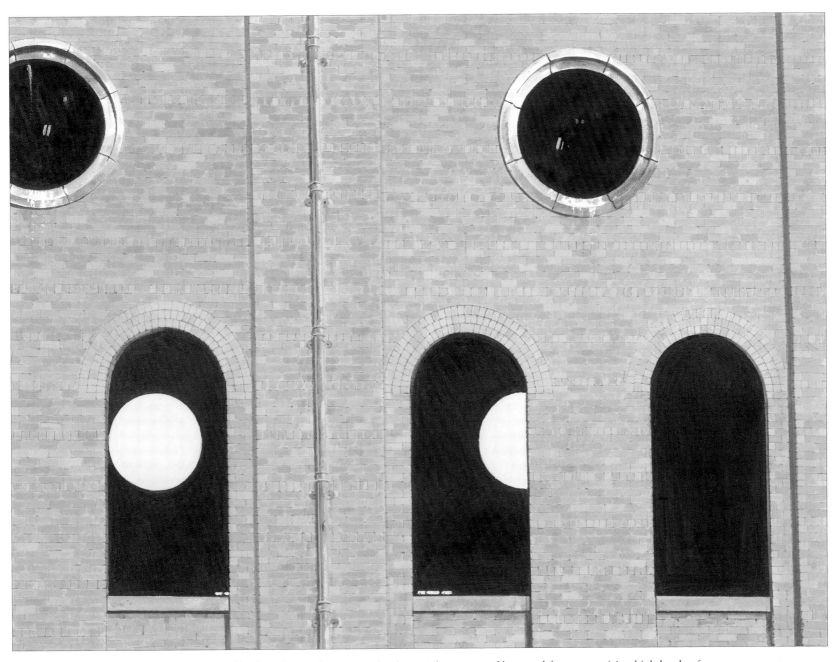

Gas production, like foundry work, generated substantial amounts of heat and fumes, requiring high levels of ventilation. The un-glazed window openings of the brick-built retort house at Gelderd Road Gasworks, Leeds, make a powerful visual statement about the 'machine age' in an architectural style we shall never see the like of again.

WORKS; and could JS be John Spink, registered as a brickmaker in South Elmsall in 1867?

The brick making industry has moved away from its 'local' roots. In the twenty-first century there are far fewer brickworks, but each is able to produce bricks in an almost infinitely varied number of colours and finishes. Eventually, the beautiful golden buff colour of sandstone will darken to almost black. But as Julius Whitehead's chimney shows, the colour of brick more easily survives the ravages of time.

BELOW LEFT The elements are slowly claiming this wooden farm cart and nineteenth century brick barn at Upper Sunnybank Farm, Birkenshaw.
BELOW Stone is used purely as decoration on Normanton Methodist Church. The abundant brick clays in the eastern part of the West Riding made it the predominant building material for towns like Normanton and Wakefield.
OPPOSITE PAGE One of the largest brick buildings in the West Riding; a six-storey warehouse built in 1871 by the North Eastern Railway at Marsh Lane, Leeds. Grain was stored in the upper floors whilst the basement and cellars contained oils and beer.

FIRE
SMOKE
AND ASHES

Could there be a more evocative description of the Industrial Revolution than the one described by George Head during his tour of the country's manufacturing districts in 1835: 'In this region of iron and coal, for the whole surface of the moor is rich in both, the approach of these foundries bears the type of universal combustion, as in the vicinity of a volcano: to witness a more awful picture, produced by the combined features of fire, smoke and ashes, an individual must bend his steps at least towards Etna or Vesuvius.'

The iron industry in West Yorkshire can be traced back to the early Middle Ages, when charcoal was used to heat the ore and extract the metal. By Tudor times the primitive blast furnaces being built were a considerable improvement on the hand and foot operated bellows previously used to raise and maintain the temperature in the smelting furnace. Until the eighteenth century, because of its dependence of supplies of timber for charcoal and water power, iron making was very much a rural industry.

The real story of iron began in Coalbrookdale, Shropshire, in

OPPOSITE PAGE The fine detailing on the decorative iron railings, Gelderd Road Gasworks, Leeds, is in sharp contrast to the workmanlike road drainage grate by Hebden Bridge iron-founders Hartley & Crabtree. BELOW An eight ton steam hammer in operation at the famous Low Moor iron works.

LEFT Halifax Borough Market, designed by local architects John and Joseph Leeming. Opened in 1898 and regarded as Yorkshires finest surviving Victorian covered market.

BELOW LEFT County Arcade, Leeds. The work of theatre designer Frank Matcham and opened in 1900. Cast-iron, glass, and colourful mosaics are supported by Burmantofts faience, a locally produced architectural ceramic found on other buildings in the Briggate area of Leeds.

OPPOSITE PAGE Iron posts have outlived the wooden cross-pieces of a decaying fence in Earlsheaton, Dewsbury.

1709, when the Quaker ironmaster Abraham Darby made one of the most significant contributions to the industrialisation of Britain, replacing charcoal by coke in the iron smelting process. Despite the vast amounts of iron and coal beneath the fields and feet of our ancestors, the shockwaves from Coalbrookdale took the best part of a century to make a significant impact on the market towns of West Yorkshire.

Three hamlets on the southern outskirts of Bradford were among the first to experience the new iron age. Emmett's, Birkenshaw in 1782, the first and smallest, followed by Bowling in 1788 and Low Moor 1791. The 'revolution' brought together entrepreneurs from all walks of life. A draper, woolstapler, solicitor and a nonconformist minister were the driving force behind the legendary iron works at Low Moor.

The Low Moor Company as it became known, grew rapidly, providing housing and schools to the town that developed around it. By making cannon and shot to fight Napoleon, both Low Moor and Bowling Iron works quickly prospered. Much later Low Moor was where the pistons and connecting rods for Brunel's great iron ship the Great Eastern were to be forged.

During the nineteenth century Britain's new industries, the machines and the buildings in which they were housed, created an insatiable demand for iron. Iron works began to appear in almost every town. Most, like Hartley and Crabtree of Hebden Bridge in the Calder Valley, supplied the needs of the local community. Beds, railings, grates, lamp posts, textile machinery and a host of everyday artefacts were their stock in trade.

Before the widespread use of steel, iron was used in an inventive and truly imaginative manner. The decorative styles favoured by artists, designers and architects found expression in iron in a way that could never be achieved in stone or brick.

This can be seen at its best in the market halls of West Yorkshire. Leeds, Dewsbury and Huddersfield all have fine examples, but without a doubt, the finest is Halifax Borough Market. The stone exterior, with its ground floor shops and typical Victorian architectural embellishments give it a certain presence in the centre of Halifax.

But it is the interior which provides the visual feast. Described as one of the finest market halls in the North of England, its richly decorated and painted ironwork supporting a lofty glazed roof provides a stunning backdrop to the building's crowning glory, the market hall clock. This wonderful timepiece has presided over the daily lives of the traders and their customers since the market was opened in 1896.

LEFT Huddersfield Wholesale Market of 1888. Recently restored, it is now an important part of the town centre.
OPPOSITE PAGE The spiral staircase at Halifax gas works survived until the 1970s. Decorative nineteenth century ironwork is now much sought after by private collectors and interior designers.

PRIDE OF PLACE

Much of the smoke and grime associated with our industrial towns came not from mill and factory chimneys, but from the thousands of fires heating the homes of our predecessors.

Coal fires conjure up images of welcome and well-being, with a tendency to overlook the daily ritual of raking out the ashes of the previous day's fire and assembling the torn newspaper, firewood and coal. It was a messy job, but the enamel hearth tin with its smooth surface was a godsend when it came to the task of clearing up.

Made of vitrified glass fused on to a metal base, the hearth tin was a close relative of the enamel signs once displayed on corner shops and railway stations. They were bought from co-ops or ironmongers and came in a variety of designs, featuring geometric and floral patterns, birds and landscapes. Christmas

OPPOSITE PAGE TOP In the days when most homes were heated by coal fires, a clean enamel hearth tin was the pride of any kitchen or front room.
OPPOSITE PAGE BOTTOM Brick & Tile Terrace, Rastrick, Brighouse.
BELOW Two chequered patterned enamel hearth tins form part of the display at an ironmonger's in Bradford Road, Dewsbury, at the turn of the twentieth century.

often marked the time for the acquisition of a new enamel hearth tin.

The demise of the fireback boiler, the 'clean-air' campaigns of the 1960s and central heating, were the downfall of this useful and decorative piece of domestic hardware. By the 1970s many could be found outside the houses where they had been lovingly cared for, covering a cellar grate or adding an extra layer of weatherproofing to an allotment shed. Like the washboard, posser and gas mantle, the enamel hearth tin has passed almost unnoticed into the rich sediment of social history.

After years of use, three enamel hearth tins create a strikingly decorative pattern over a cellar grate outside a house in Mirfield.

CROWNING GLORY

Chimney pots no longer seem to be part of an architect's visual vocabulary. In the nineteenth century, builders of the humblest row of cottages or terrace houses would fit a set of shapely, fluted chimney pots to crown their work. These were usually chosen from a sample book showing a company's range of designs. Julius Whitehead's Fireclay Works, Clayton near Bradford, produced drainage pipes but also had a more visible line of products in chimney pots. Did chimney pot designers always put function before form in order to catch the eye of builders and architects?

The phrase 'variations on a theme' could have been coined to describe chimney pots. Round, square or octagonal in section. Fluted, with an infinite variety of slats, holes and sawtooth crowns, it is little wonder that quite a few have been brought down to earth to host a cornucopia of busy lizzies and fuchsias in gardens. Despite progress, there are thankfully still enough around to bring variety and interest to the skylines of our towns and cities.

ABOVE A page from the sample book of Julius Whitehead's clay pipe and fireclay works, Clayton, Bradford.
LEFT Looking like the targets of a fairground stall. Five out of six chimney pots in Wharfe Street, Bradford await their final demise.

OPPOSITE PAGE The chimney pots on one of a row of terrace houses in Holbeck, Leeds.
ABOVE RIGHT 'Where does all the smoke go?' The mysteries of the chimney being explained by a Bradford chimney sweep in the 1920s
RIGHT With battered flutes and crowns, five Batley chimney pots await their fate.

HOME
NUMBER

Numbers are becoming increasingly important in our everyday lives. In the past it was sufficient to remember the number of the bus into town, your co-op 'divi' cheque number, school register number; and who in the armed forces ever forgot their roll number?

Door numbers; written on envelopes and searched out by visitors and postmen, are a small but crucial link between the houses we live in and the rest of the world. Discreet oval enamel plates, raised cast metal numerals, or more decoratively, part of a leaded glass fanlight; these numerical gems, mere details in the streetscape, bring a touch of individuality to one of the most ordinary but important aspects of our lives.

ABOVE Enamel door number plate, Fitzwilliam Street, Huddersfield.
BELOW LEFT Decorative leaded fanlight, Ovenden, Halifax.
BELOW RIGHT Leeds Road, Bradford.

The front door of an abandoned single storey miner's cottage in Towngate, Wyke, near Bradford.

A STONE'S
THROW AWAY

D riven by the rapid growth of industry, the population of the West Riding increased dramatically in the nineteenth century. By the end of the century our towns and cities had well-developed commercial hearts. Town halls, libraries, market halls, theatres, technical colleges, hospitals, shops, offices and banks became working monuments to civic pride. If these grand buildings were the visible superstructure of a flourishing society, then the mills and factories surrounding them were the engine house driving its prosperity.

The River Aire and the railway lines running east to west provided a buffer zone between Leeds' commercial centre and its southern flank, where fire-belching foundries and heavy engineering works produced the steam engines, ploughs and locomotives that made the city famous. Bradford's mills and warehouses came right into the heart of the city, whilst the mines

South Parade, Halifax. 1967.

Amongst the houses dyeworks owner J.E. Wainhouse built for his Halifax workforce was Wainhouse Terrace,
an unusual row of back-to-back houses. A tower enclosed stairs leading to a gallery running above
under-dwellings giving access to the houses at the rear.

and iron works at Bowling and Low Moor were themselves only a few miles distant on the outskirts.

Halifax came tumbling down the slopes from Pellon with ever increasing density to the foot of Beacon Hill, where the waters of Hebble Brook sought refuge beside railway lines, gasworks, carpet and worsted mills. The worsted mills that made Huddersfield's reputation, supported by dye works and iron works, ran along the banks of the Colne and Holme.

On the edge of Yorkshire's largest coalfield and on the banks of the River Calder, stood Wakefield, where malthouses and

Sharlston, near Wakefield. Typical miners' houses in the Yorkshire coalfield.

breweries took in grain from barges plying the Calder & Hebble Navigation Canal. Dirt and grime, the unintentional bye-products of manufacturing, became an accepted fact of life, but matters of public health and town planning were not high on the agendas of the building clubs and speculative builders of houses for the workers and their families. Single room cottages and back-to-back houses created a maze of alleyways and courtyards with crude sanitation and drainage. It took several Improvement

Acts to raise the standards of planning and house building. Back-to-back houses continued to be built throughout Victorian times, but the Leeds Improvement Act of 1866 restricted their construction to blocks of eight in an attempt to allow in more light and air.

A more responsible and philanthropic outlook was shared by early building co-operatives and building societies, and by some mill owners; notably Sir Titus Salt, who in 1860 created a model village for the workpeople of his alpaca mill at Saltaire on the outskirts of Bradford. Other similar developments were built throughout the West Riding. On a smaller scale, J. E. Wainhouse, whose dyeworks chimney still dominates the Halifax skyline, built homes for his workforce that included a fine terrace of houses with a rear gallery overlooking the Calder Valley.

There was tremendous loyalty among railway companies and their employees. The Midland Railway built houses at Normanton and Bradford. The station and engine shed at Low Moor have long since gone, but a row of houses built by the Lancashire & Yorkshire Railway still survives.

As the Yorkshire coalfield began to develop, colliery owners built houses to attract the labour force required to exploit the area's rich coal seams. In New Sharlston a terrace of 55 houses became one of the longest in Britain.

For most town and city dwellers in the past, the proximity between home life and place of work was important. Corner shop, school, public house, church or chapel were always close at hand. In a world of washing lines and comparatively little traffic, children's played hopscotch, hide and seek, football and cricket. Street traders; milkmen, 'rag and bone' men, ice-cream vendors and fruit and vegetables sold from a horse and cart, meant that streets were rarely quiet.

Despite clearance and redevelopment much still remains, with conspicuous additions from the world's car manufacturers and television companies reminding us that the world's longest running weekly television drama was founded on street culture.

The topography of the West Riding and the piecemeal methods of some builders often produced highly individual examples of domestic architecture, like the appropriately named Coffin End, Thornton, on the outskirts of Bradford.

TOP Terrace houses cluster round a mill in Batley Carr.
ABOVE The Lancashire & Yorkshire Railway emerged from Beacon Hill Tunnel to
carve a path between Baldwin Terrace and Clark Bridge worsted mill, Halifax.

Raglan Street, Halifax. Those living in the street a century ago probably worked in a toffee factory, dye works, worsted or cotton mills – all of which were within a stone's throw.

In the early part of the nineteenth century, before the development of the Yorkshire coalfield, mining was on a much smaller scale. Many miners and their families lived in single storey cottages like these at Wyke on the southern edge of Bradford.

Many of the larger railway companies provided housing for their employees. Built by the
Lancashire and Yorkshire Railway, Railway Terrace, Low Moor, overlooked the engine shed and
railway station, both of which were demolished in the late 1960's.

MONARCHS
ADMIRALS
&COMMONERS

Bean, Acorn, Cranberry, Wheat, Bread, Apple; not the ingredients for a summer picnic, but street names from the Burmantofts area of Leeds at the turn of the twentieth century. House building on an unprecedented scale had by then created a maze of roads and streets. Each had to be identified with a suitable name. Many houses were built in blocks creating the opportunity for a sequence. Builders often named a group of streets after members of their families; Alice, Stanley, Catherine, William, Henry. Admirals and battles seemed to capture the imagination; Nelson and Trafalgar in particular. The names of trees, flowers, and birds; subjects close to Victorian and Edwardian hearts and homes, were chosen, no doubt influenced by the fashionably decorative styles of the Art Nouveau and Arts and Crafts Movements.

The railways now covered the country, extending personal and commercial boundaries. Place names outside the West Riding, like Sunderland, Berwick, Folkestone and Northumberland achieved a permanence in the streets of our own towns and cities. Then there were the names which alluded to traditional Victorian values; Temperance, Perseverance, Industrial, Hope, and Union.

Cast iron was the principal material for street signs, but enamel and ceramic could also be found. More uniquely, in the Low Moor and Wibsey area of south Bradford signs were hand painted on slate, some surviving well beyond the 1970s.

Saints and prime ministers were also commemorated. But it was the Queen and her consort who most found favour with planners and builders. In 2001, a century after her death, there still remain 47 Victoria Streets and 31 Victoria Roads in West Yorkshire.

OPPOSITE PAGE A selection of street signs.
Sycamore Street, Wakefield (ceramic tiles); Morton Street, Ovenden, Halifax (enamel); Oldham Street, Brighouse (cast iron); H. Elliot, Grove Street, Ovenden, Halifax (carved stone); Huddersfield Road, Wyke (painted slate); off Commercial Street, Batley (cast iron).

SPENDING
A PENNY

It now seems incredible, but only forty years ago, when four mop-haired young men from Liverpool were taking the world of popular music by storm, a goodly proportion of the population regularly left the comfort of their homes to 'spend a penny'. This meant picking up a key on a loop of string before taking a short walk across a yard to a group of outbuildings. Water closets, which were often placed near ashpits, came into general use in the mid-nineteenth century, but Victorian house builders seemed reluctant to bring them indoors.

Shared external toilets saved valuable space during the house building boom. Though lime-washed and as clean as the furnished room you had just left, the outside toilet was totally devoid of any creature comforts. In winter a slow burning paraffin lamp with its distinctive 'aroma' and eerie yellow light guarded against frozen pipes. The 'convenience' itself would have been a direct descendent of Alexander Cummings' flushing toilet with overhead cistern patented in 1775.

A much more basic design could also still be found as late as the 1960s. This was the 'tippler'. Out of sight, beneath its simple bench-like seat, water would be constantly flowing into a kind of hopper which, when full, would automatically tip the water down the soil pipe. As the user had no control over the timing, the sudden gush of water from the flushing action could come as quite a surprise!

Back-to-back with an ash-pit in between, nature slowly encroaches on a pair of outside toilets in Thornton Road, Bradford.

'The 'Rock, Wash Down' and 'The Clencher'. Brand names from an altogether different age; dreamed up in the board rooms of companies like J. Duckett & Son Ltd. Burnley, sanitary-ware suppliers to the builders of Upper Spen Buildings, Gomersal, near Cleckheaton.

A group of gable-end toilets and ash-pits in Thornton, Bradford.

Multi-storeyed back-to-back houses with under-dwellings were common on the steep hillsides of the Calder Valley, creating these unusual double-decker outside toilets at Woodhouse Terrace near Sowerby Bridge.

OUT OF TUNE

Long gone are the days when it seemed that every other house had a piano or harmonium, and a stack of sheet music ranging from Parry's 'Jerusalem' to Johnny Ray.

Victorian hymn writers and the music hall were very much behind the piano's popular appeal in the late nineteenth century, fuelling the live musical traditions associated with the church, chapels, Sunday schools and public houses.

Piano lessons were almost obligatory if you lived in a house with an upright in the front room. With its iron frame, burr walnut outer case, and panelling decorated with intricate marquetry, few could resist a rendering of 'chopsticks'.

In the 1960s stereo sound brought the magic of a live performance to our living rooms. The piano, which, even as a piece of furniture always had a presence in our homes, became unloved, un-tuned and took up too much room. Slum clearance programmes provided the finale to many of these once prized and polished instruments – many of which were left behind to the mercies of the demolition gang when their owners realised that their new home would be sixteen floors up in a high-rise tower block.

OPPOSITE PAGE A Sunday in 1974. The Salvation Army Band plays for the residents of Danube Grove, Wortley, Leeds. The houses have since been replaced by a car dealership and industrial units.
ABOVE Few pianos made the move from the terrace to the high-rise. Here the last remaining brick terrace houses in the Little London area of Leeds are dwarfed by the tower blocks built to replace them.
RIGHT The Royal Warrant did not save this Victorian 'upright', which I found abandoned in the front room of a derelict house in Beeston, Leeds.

LOST
LOCK-UPS

A lock-up shelters beneath a railway viaduct at the bottom of Clifton Common, Brighouse. The viaduct, built by the Lancashire & Yorkshire Railway in 1881, survived a further twenty years after the line it carried closed in 1952. The wooden lock-up is still serving it's twenty-first century customers.

Though its origins go back beyond Victorian times, the wooden lock-up shop personifies both community and individuality as much as any aspect of our society. These fast disappearing establishments readily took root in the odd corners and spaces created by the seemingly random expansion of towns and cities. Most commodities were sold from lock-ups: fish and chips, pie and peas, tripe, groceries, newspapers, not to mention tattoos and hair cuts.

Many wooden lock-ups seemed to belong to cobblers, harking back to the days when boots and shoes were made and repaired locally. Because the shop was also the workplace, customers and passers-by would, even yards from the doorway, pick up the pungent smell of newly tanned leather. As well as the proprietor

and his wife, there lived behind the counter of a cobbler's lock-up near Heckmondwike a magnificent parrot in a large wire cage. Well-versed in the technical vocabulary of shoe repairing, it became a great attraction to customers and their children.

One shop keeper who opened a wooden lock up in Guiseley near Leeds in 1928 became a household, and eventually an international name. Harry Ramsden's is synonymous with the finest portions of that national delicacy, fish and chips. His original wooden lock-up can still be found in the grounds of the current more palatial restaurant

By the 1970s nature had begun to take over the entrance to boot maker, Stanley Addy's long abandoned wooden lock-up in Bridge Road, Bradley on the outskirts of Huddersfield.

Gelderd Road, Birstall.

Fish, rabbits and poultry could be bought from The Bargate Fisheries, the archetypal wooden lock-up shop in Manchester Road, Linthwaite.

ABOVE Yorkshire's most famous wooden lock-up. Harry Ramsden's original fish and chip shop of 1928, still preserved beside its more palatial successor at Guiseley near Leeds.
LEFT The Master Craftsman. A cobbler in his lock-up shop in Churwell Hill, Leeds.
OPPOSITE PAGE 'Pie & Peas'. The last days of a wooden lock-up in a decaying corner of Wyke, Bradford.

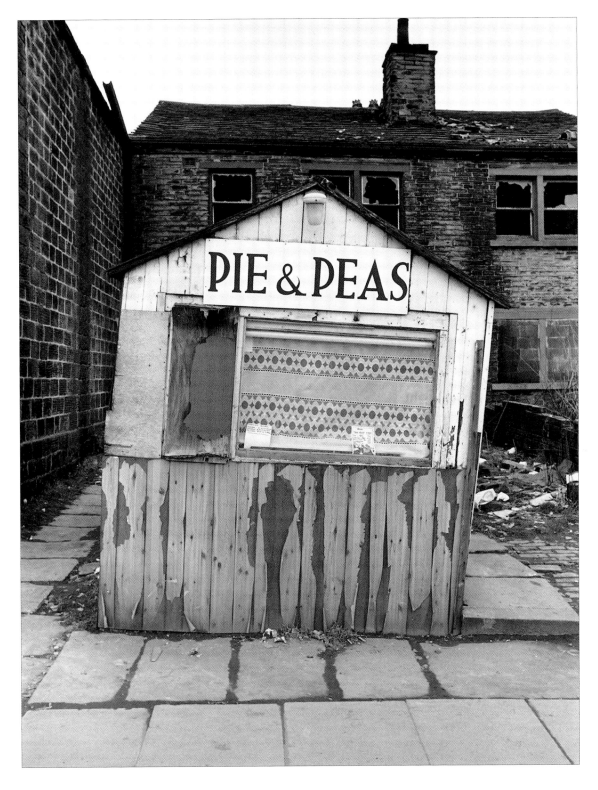

A NATION OF SHOPKEEPERS

Until the 1970s, out of town shopping meant something completely different to the brightly lit, air conditioned all-under-one-roof experience of today.

On either side of the roads leading into towns, ran a ribbon of shops; grocers, newsagents, opticians, butchers, bakers, tailors, milliners, off-licences, chemists, barbers, pet-shops and post offices. The list is endless and ran in a repeating pattern of seemingly infinite permutations. Dewsbury Road, Manchester Road, Leeds Road, Westgate, Northgate. Names with a sense of place, direction and purpose, each an opportunity to attract passing trade, but above all representing the visible face of the

Melias Tea Stores, Crackenedge Lane, Dewsbury, in 1910.

The vitrified glass coating on enamel signs helped their survival, as on this Lyons' Tea sign on a derelict corner shop at Hill Top, Low Moor.

Shops line Northgate and Northumberland Street, Huddersfield, in 1959. Most disappeared with the construction of the town's inner ring road.

communities in the rows of streets and houses behind them.

The diversity of shops was matched by the variety of shop fronts, many with retractable canvas awnings to prevent sunlight from fading their window displays. This was an area of suburbia where, if you looked closely enough, among the fresh bread, meat, fruit, vegetables and daily newspapers, you could find more than a few leftovers from yesteryear's retailing history. Decorative shop doorways with the original proprietors' names set in their mosaic floors. Enamel or metal signs, with an almost indestructible coating of vitrified glass, advertising Parkinson's Pills, Lyons' Tea, Colman's Starch or Reckitt's Bag Blue, looking almost as new as the day they were put there, maybe fifty years earlier. At eye-level or just above, a four foot metal thermometer

advertised Stephens' Inks, 'for all temperatures' – and now a valuable collector's item.

Gable ends facing the traffic on the busier streets displayed painted signs advertising local shops and services, along with familiar household names; Spratt's Bonio dog food, Bile Beans, Park Drive cigarettes, Ramsden's Stone Trough Ales. All probably the work of a local signwriter and housepainter. Along with the then familiar Turog and Hovis Bread gold-painted wooden signs outside the local bakers, such streets presented a curious mixture of local surnames and well-known brand names.

Shopping then had a more fundamental purpose. Corner shopkeepers, whose families lived above or behind the shop, were your neighbours and staple providers. Your local grocer would have a discreet working knowledge of the contents of your pantry through a regular weekly order delivered to your door by an assistant. Many shopkeepers were willing to provide

Swags of grapes and a Cadburys sign greeted customers to a corner shop in Armley Road, Leeds, for almost a century.

goods 'on tick' through mutual trust.

In the days before pocket calculators, bar-codes and decimalisation, the corner shopkeeper would take a pencil, usually from behind his ear, and on a plain white paper bag or sheet of grease-proof paper, and with considerably underplayed panache, reckon up your shopping bill in pounds, shillings and pence. It was done in seconds, and was rarely wrong!

Food rationing in Britain continued for some time after the war. Despite the shortages Sainsbury's opened their first self-service 'Q-less shopping' store in 1950 in Croydon. Most goods were pre-packed and priced and the 'store' heralded other new innovations pointing to the future; refrigerated displays and shopping with a wire basket.

It was the mid-1960s before the first supermarkets opened their doors in West Yorkshire, to customers who probably approached this new style of shopping with cautious curiosity.

Within a decade curiosity had turned to conversion. The supermarket was becoming the way to shop, the car the way to travel. Town planners got out their blue pencils to sketch the latest version of post-war Utopia. Inner ring roads and dual carriageways swept all before them, and in the dust fell row upon row of corner shops.

Memories of corner shops and co-ops bring to mind the fearsomely efficient hand cranked bacon slicer. A muted clanking sound accompanied its relentless rhythmic swishing as it sliced through a ham or a side of bacon. Many corner shops have survived. But the unrelenting march of progress took more than a slice or two out of a way of life that owed more to personal service than style and presentation.

Victorian wood and plasterwork. A shop doorway awaits demolition in Manningham Lane, Bradford.

TOP Once an important part of village life, by 1974 Howden Clough Post Office near Batley was waiting to be converted into a private house.
ABOVE Wind and rain sweeping down the Colne Valley from the moors above Huddersfield have left a single Art Nouveau tile on a butcher's shop in Milnsbridge virtually untouched.

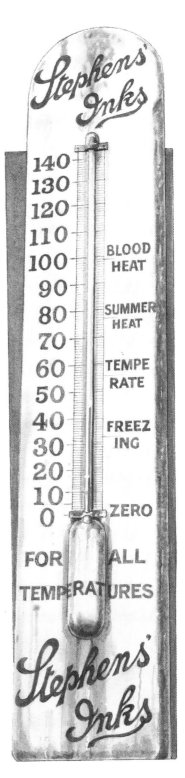

ABOVE Many corner shops today are run by Asian families, who have added a variety of exotic fruits and vegetables to our High Street shopping lists.
RIGHT A four feet high metal thermometer advertising Stephens' inks, Lockwood Road, Huddersfield.

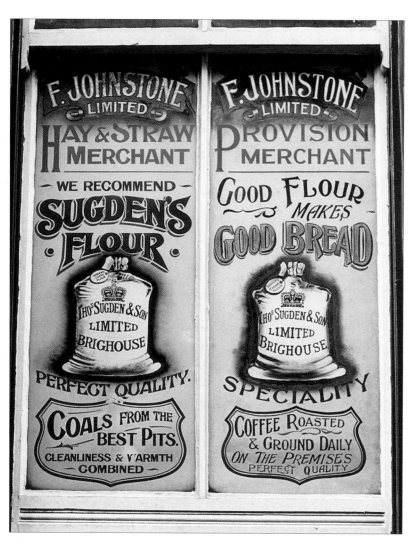

Straw, flour, bread, coffee and coal; basic commodities from the days before seemingly unlimited choice, advertised on a window in Marsden in the 1970s.

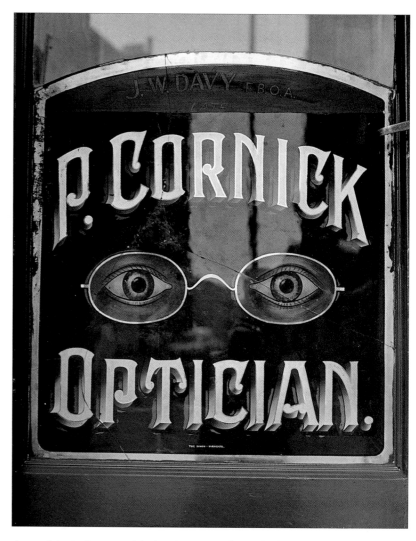

An optician's doorway, Market Street, Heckmondwike.

A gypsy and his horse and cart trot past a row of derelict shops in Holbeck Lane, Leeds, in 1973.

UNION IS STRENGTH

'The Greatest Economic Movement of Modern Times for the benefit of the People', the aims and objects of the Bradford Co-operative Society sum up the profound influence the Co-operative movement had on the lives of ordinary people and the history of retail trading.

Robert Owen, a mill owner and visionary Socialist, is recognised as the architect of Co-operative commonwealth. The Industrial Revolution generated prosperity for some, but little in the way of material wealth for the majority. Owens' ideal of sharing for the common good was taken up by societies formed in the late 1820s to provide the basic commodities of life at prices affordable to the working man.

In 1827 The Meltham Mills Society on the outskirts of Huddersfield briefly flourished. But the true birthplace of the Co-operative movement belongs to a Lancashire cotton town, where on a Saturday evening in 1844 the Rochdale Equitable Pioneers opened their first shop to its first customer, an old lady who bought half-a-pound of sugar.

LEFT The grocery department of Brighouse Co-operative Society's main branch in the 1920s.
BELOW 'Union is Strength', Queensbury

'Sharing for the common good'. The beehive meaningfully symbolised the Co-operative Movement's philosophy.

The Co-operative philosophy was based on the principle of membership for all, with returns on the profits payable as a dividend on the amount spent on purchases. Members were given a number, which would be quoted when paying for goods at the till, in the knowledge that for every pound spent, the pennies would be building up into a nest-egg for 'divi' day. Many people could still remember their Co-op number long after the introduction of trading stamps in the 1960s.

The principle of working together for the common good and sharing the benefits appealed to the movement's predominantly working class membership, to whom loyalty to their employers, religious beliefs, pub, cricket or football team was often a foregone conclusion. It is easy to see why the beehive symbol came to be displayed over the entrance to some branches of the Co-op, often supported by the words Co-operative Industrial Society or the phrase 'Union is Strength'.

By the latter half of the nineteenth century the larger towns had set up sizeable Co-op shops and offices supporting branches in outlying villages. One West Riding Society was set up in 1859 with twelve shillings left over from a tea party. By the 1920s the co-operative movement as a whole had become the largest wholesale and retail organisation in Britain, moving into every aspect of retailing with the support of its own factories, mills, farms and ships – even tea estates in India. The Co-op pre-empted supermarket 'own-label' branding by several decades. Banking, insurance, and welfare schemes were also part of the Co-op's far reaching empire.

Despite its size, the Co-operative movement engendered tremendous loyalty. Every Co-op branch, and there were thousands, were establishments of great individuality and an important part of the community. The resounding sound of 'Union is Strength' suggests a guarantee of immortality. But changes in society can often out-run ideologies, and the Co-operative movement founded on 'community values' lost out to a society that places greater emphasis on individual freedom.

OPPOSITE PAGE Bradford Road, Brighouse.
ABOVE Morley.
ABOVE RIGHT Clifton, near Brighouse.

VICTORIA'S SHOPPING MALL

Flora and Pomona gazed down on Bradford's shoppers for almost a century. Two seldom noticed carved stone figures by William Day Keyworth, representing the goddesses of flowers and fruit, they were part of the decorative stonework above the main entrance to Bradford's Kirkgate Market.

The Market opened in 1878, after being built to a competition winning design by Bradford architects Lockwood and Mawson, a partnership that well and truly left its mark on the city. Other buildings of theirs to survive include St. George's Hall (1853), Titus Salt's mill, Saltaire (1853), The Wool Exchange (1867) and City Hall (1873).

Kirkgate Market, like its contemporaries in other West Riding towns, was the one-stop shopping centre of its day. Markets have been a central part of town life since the Middle Ages. The large indoor markets pioneered by the Victorians retained the spirit of their medieval predecessors but brought a more permanent solution to the business of market trading.

Despite its size, it seems almost churlish to suggest that outwardly Bradford's Kirkgate Market hall was anything special. At ground level there were shops facing Kirkgate, Darley Street and Godwin Street. The main entrance in Kirkgate led through to a set of iron gates made by the famous Coalbrookdale Company, then up a flight of stone steps to a set of wooden doors surmounted by a glass screen with notices earnestly requesting you to refrain from the dangerous and objectionable habit of spitting! A further flight of steps took you to the market hall itself.

A photograph taken at the turn of the century shows the market hall as a lively place with all the atmosphere and clutter of an outdoor market. Early electric lighting pendants hang from the ornate ironwork.

Memories of Kirkgate Market from the 1950s are more down to earth. The same ornate ironwork provided a canopy to rows of more 'robust' looking stalls than the ones in the Edwardian

LEFT The Kirkgate entrance to Bradford's Kirkgate Market.
OPPOSITE PAGE The art deco movement left its fingerprints on the market's Victorian interior when some of the cafés around its interior were 'modernised' in the years between the wars. M.J. Armitage's cafe provided shoppers with welcome refreshment and a brief respite.

One of the original gas lamps stands in front of the fine proportions and workmanship of the glazed oak screen at the Kirkgate entrance. Beyond are the iron gates made by the Coalbrookdale Company.

photograph. Here, gathered under one roof were the purveyors of life's essentials; pots, pans, clothes, prams, curtains and fabrics, books old and new, even a toy shop where a few shillings earned on a paper round could be spent on adding to your collection of 'Meccano' and 'Dinky' toys. The weary shopper could find rest and refreshment in one of the cafés around its perimeter. Some, like Craven and Armitage, acquired art-deco frontages contrasting incongruously with the building's ornate ironwork.

The austerity of the war years gave planners and designers the impetus to make a fresh start. Thankfully, Bradford escaped the 'blitz' relatively unscathed. But the 1960s saw Bradford embrace the word 'modernisation' in a big way. City centres became the province of the retailers whose branches and brand-names were as familiar in Kent as they were in Yorkshire.

Although covered markets have survived elsewhere, Kirkgate Market found itself out of step with Bradford's new air of consumer optimism. Its heart was still in the right place, but a decade of neglect brought it to its last week in November 1973 looking decidedly unkempt, if not unloved. Demolition began immediately, Bradford really couldn't wait for Kirkgate Market's bright new successor, and the only logical replacement to the cause of one stop shopping – a shopping mall.

ABOVE A message you wouldn't expect to find in one of today's shopping malls.

RIGHT The unique atmosphere of a Victorian covered market is captured in this 1904 photograph of Bradford's Kirkgate Market.

A busy Saturday morning in Kirkgate Market in 1973, but closure and demolition are no more than a week away.

The same view a week later, the noise of demolition echoes round the market's cathedral like interior.

A JOB
FOR LIFE

Until the 1960s it must have seemed to many that the mill wheels of Yorkshire's West Riding would turn forever. Railway engines, cars, chemicals, leather, wire, biscuits and toffee were also produced in this part of the county; but it is the mills and the textile industry that will be forever associated with the industrial West Riding. Giant mills like the ones built by Samuel Cunliffe Lister and Titus Salt in Bradford, and Crossley's carpet factory in Halifax, dominated the landscape and the lives of generations of the men and women who worked in them.

The textile industry in its hey-day was all-encompassing. The mills in towns like Cleckheaton produced woollen yarn, whilst in Brighouse, a few miles away in the Calder valley, silk and cotton predominated. Leeds was famous for tailoring and ready-made clothing, and was an early centre for flax spinning.

The working lives of thousands of people in Dewsbury and Batley were assured when in 1813 Benjamin Law, a Batley clothier, discovered shoddy, a fairly coarse but hard-wearing cloth made by re-weaving shredded woollen rags. Mungo, or ground rags mixed with virgin wool and pioneered by Law's

LEFT The small building with the lantern roof on the right of the photograph is all that now remains of Prospect Mills, Sowerby Bridge.
BELOW Steam powered some mills until their final closure. Walker's Mill, Mirfield, 1971.

The Colne Valley brought the river, canal and railway down from the Pennine town of Marsden into Huddersfield. Once a cotton spinning and warping mill, with a capacity of 52,000 spindles, Britannia Mills was one of the many that filled the valley floor until the decline of the textile industry saw the closure and demolition of this and other mills in the Colne Valley in the 1970s and '80s.

nephew in 1834, produced a much finer cloth. 'Shoddy' and 'mungo' became part of the vocabulary of the West Riding, as did 'tops and noils', 'slubbing and dyeing', 'twisting and spinning'.

The Yorkshire textile industry still produces some of the finest cloth in the world. In lamenting its decline, it is easy to forget the years of misery and deprivation that followed the introduction of the factory system; the mills where children as young as seven often worked twelve hours a day. The 1847 Factory Act was the first step to improving conditions, but even in the early twentieth century girls of twelve began working as half-timers, starting at six in the morning and finishing at 12.30 before spending the afternoon at school.

These were the days of the 'knocker-up', whose job it was to patrol the streets in the early mornings, tapping on bedroom windows with a long pole to ensure the occupants made it to the mill. Late arrivals were often locked out until 8.30, or breakfast time, with the subsequent loss of earnings.

The most striking thing about the West Ridings mills was the continuous metallic clatter of dozens of spinning frames, or power looms taking their power from overhead line shafts and belting. Spinners and weavers soon learned the art of lip-reading. The ingrained smell of oil and wool grease hit you as soon as you walked in.

ABOVE The face of experience. A Batley spinner.
LEFT A wool weighing scale made by J. Brayshaw & Son, Bradford, in the warehouse of George Anderton and Son, Victoria Mills, Cleckheaton.
OPPOSITE PAGE The year is 1980, but time appears to have stood still on the top floor of a woollen mill in Batley Carr.

Conditions slowly improved; few mill owners were true tyrants, and there were some whose social consciences matched their entrepreneurial skills, creating not only decent housing for their workforces, but schools churches, chapels, hospitals, institutes and civic buildings.

Large mills were the 'mother-ships' to whole communities, dictating the rhythm of life to hundreds. For two weeks a year in the summer, the mills and surrounding town would fall silent during the annual migration to the coast. There was also the traditional 'mill trip' when the entire workforce, including the directors, would board special trains bound for Blackpool or Scarborough.

The influx of cheaper goods from abroad and the develop-ment of man-made fibres began to have an impact on Yorkshire's textile industry. Many mills were equipped with machinery that had been 'built to last' in the early part of the twentieth century, but was woefully inefficient when compared to the machines emerging from Europe. Continental shift patterns were tried but came too late to save many companies, and by the 1970s many mills were lying derelict or facing demolition. Mill buildings that survived experienced a metamorphosis from manufacturing to 'servicing and distribution'. Split into smaller units; graphic designers, photographers, public relations companies and craft workshops moved in. Computers, telephones and fax machines now stand where carding, spinning and weaving machinery rattled and clattered for over a century.

Clocks and bell cupolas were features of some early West Riding mills; Black Dyke Mills, Queensbury, 1832, and (OPPOSITE PAGE) Bowling Mills Combing Company, Manchester Road, Bradford.

ABOVE Mill girls at James Sykes Mill, Milnsbridge, celebrate the Coronation in June 1953.
OPPOSITE PAGE Said to be the largest silk mill in the world at the time of it's construction in 1873. A bird's eye view of
Samuel Lister's Manningham Mills, Bradford, with it's 249 foot high Italianate chimney.

SPLENDOUR IN THE SKY

Until the 1960s the skyline of most textile towns was a forest of mill chimneys. Almost all have now disappeared, along with the mills for which they helped provide the power.

The mill chimney was a unique creation of the age of coal and steam. Its height was related more to the strength of the draught required to maintain a good fire to raise a powerful head of steam, than to any wish to keep smoke and soot away from washing lines below. This association with dirt and grime has blackened the character of something which often had real

architectural merit; albeit a few hundred feet above eye level.

Square, round or octagonal; most were as unpretentiously functional in design and decoration as the mills they were part of. But some things in our industrial surroundings were always destined to be embellished with more than purely functional attributes. Samuel Cunliffe Lister's imposing chimney still towers over his former silk mill in Manningham, Bradford, and the Calder Valley would be much the poorer without the monumental presence of John Edward Wainhouse's dye works chimney. These worthy giants tend to overshadow their less ostentatious brethren, many of whom are no longer with us, but are surely amongst the most neglected aspects of our industrial past.

LEFT TO RIGHT Dean Clough Mills, Halifax; Valley Mills, Elland (demolished): Clarence Mills, Cleckheaton (demolished): Henry Burrows, Batley Carr (demolished): Spafield Mills, Elland (demolished): Waterfield Mills, Cleckheaton (demolished): Wortley Fireclay Company, Leeds (demolished): Whetley Mills, Bradford.

THREADS OF FORTUNE

The eighteenth century Halifax Piece Hall is now the only surviving example of a unique group of buildings, the market halls where the woollen cloth woven in the West Riding was finally sold.

After a hand loom weaver completed a woollen 'piece' it was taken to a fulling mill, where the loose fabric was soaked in soap and water, trampled under foot or pounded by water-powered fulling stocks – large wooden hammers which beat the cloth until the fibres blended together to produce a smoother, thicker material. The cloth was dried on tenterhooks and brushed with teasels before being cropped with huge shears. The finished piece was then sold at the weekly market. Originally cloth markets were held in the open air; as for example in the churchyard of Huddersfield parish church.

Both woollen and worsted (where the wool is both carded and combed) trades began to expand rapidly in the eighteenth century. Churchyards and streets, always at the mercy of the elements, became inadequate as market places. Small cloth halls began to be built. But it was the Leeds Mixed or Coloured Cloth Hall of 1758, then the largest building in Leeds, which became the first of a new generation of market halls, followed by Huddersfield (1766), Bradford (1773), Leeds White Cloth Hall (1775), Wakefield (1778), and Halifax Piece Hall (1779).

All the cloth or piece halls had rooms for rent, where clothiers' could display their finished pieces, and a bell signal led the hours of trading. Impressive though these buildings were, their working lives as early showcases of the West Riding cloth trade were relatively short. Even as the cloth halls were being built, inventors and engineers were working on the successors to spinning wheels and wooden hand looms.

The mechanisation of the textile industry meant that the manufacturing processes were concentrated into single buildings – the mills – where mill owners could do business with

The Halifax Piece Hall of 1779 is now the only surviving example of the West Riding's Georgian cloth markets.

32-40 Station Road, Batley. Severely damaged by fire in 1982 it is nevertheless a Grade II listed building

32-40 Station Road, Batley. An impressive crescent of selling houses, where buyers could view the cloth, was completed in 1887 by the Taylor family, when the town's reputation as a producer of shoddy cloth was reaching its height. The Moorish architectural details above the doors and windows reflected the town's worldwide trading links, and are reminiscent of the Bradford Wool Exchange, completed in 1867.

merchants. By the middle of the nineteenth century, as mill building reached its peak, cloth and piece halls had become an outmoded way of trading.

The expanding railway network provided mobility to merchants and buyers, as well as the means to transport raw materials and finished products. Competition became more intense as markets grew wider. Merchants and manufacturers began to realise the value of style and presentation to their potential customers, especially in the warehouses where their products were stored and sold.

The second half of the nineteenth century witnessed the great era in textile warehouse building in the West Riding. The confidence and showmanship inherent in merchandising began to manifest itself in wool warehouses. This was not confined only to the high quality worsted trade. The shoddy cloth manufacturers of Batley and Dewsbury shared similar notions of architectural grandeur as consignments of rags came into their mills from all over the world, much of it to be turned into a hard wearing cloth particularly suitable for military uniforms. Ironically, business boomed as a result of the many wars fought in the nineteenth century, including the Crimean and American Civil Wars. Dewsbury and Batley's finest buildings are without a doubt their wool warehouses, situated in both towns near their respective railway stations. Many of these have survived the decline of the shoddy wool industry since the Second World War.

Fire, a constant threat to mills and warehouses, almost claimed a particularly impressive crescent of selling houses in Station Road, Batley, when in 1982 the entire centre section was destroyed. Built between 1860 and 1887 by the Taylor family, the crescent, like other buildings in the area, was richly decorated with carved foliage and animals. Window and door arches in alternate red and cream sandstone suggest a Moorish influence reminiscent of Bradford's Wool Exchange of 1867. Even in its present semi-derelict state it still remains an impressive building, fully justifying its Grade II Listed status.

'Indeed there is nothing that can be spun and woven that does not come to Bradford'. The words of J.B. Priestley neatly sum up that city's pre-eminence in the worsted trade. Bradford's industrial and commercial growth throughout the nineteenth century encompassed all the traditional textile manufacturing processes as well as leading the way in others.

Titus Salt pioneered the commercial applications of alpaca and mohair combined with cotton to create what are termed 'Lustre Fabrics'. Another of Bradford's great textile geniuses, E. Cunliffe Lister, built Manningham Mills, one of the largest in the West Riding, to produce silks and velvets.

These fine fashion fabrics attracted European merchants, from Germany in particular, whose experience in export markets world-wide made a vital contribution to the commercial life of the city. Between 1855 and 1873, in an area between Leeds Road and the parish church, a whole community dedicated to Bradford's mercantile progress was created. Here in Little Germany, as the area became known, were chapels, schools, a Temperance Hall and arguably, the finest group of textile warehouses in Britain.

Most of the buildings were the work of Bradford's most eminent architectural partnerships, Lockwood and Mawson, and Milnes and France. Richly decorated with neo-classical or Italianate frontages, their fine craftsmanship is continued in the decorative wood and plasterwork of the interiors. There may well have been a handfull of hand-loom weavers still working in outlying hamlets in the middle of the nineteenth century, but it was in the raucous centre of Bradford that Yorkshire's textile industry reached its peak.

The dust begins to settle on a part of Dewsbury's distinguished textile past, in the entrance to a wool warehouse in Wellington Road.

ABOVE Countless streets, roads, parks and mills commemorated the name of Britain's longest reigning monarch. A carving of Queen
Victoria's head crowned the doorway to Victoria Warehouse, Batley, until it's destruction by fire in the 1980s.
OPPOSITE PAGE Wellington Road Dewsbury. Nineteenth century majolica tiles, their design influenced by the Arts and Crafts
movement, display a richness of decoration once found in the humblest of wool warehouses.

ABOVE The skeletal remains of Ormondroyd's warehouse in 1973, when many Bradford warehouses were demolished
to make way for the city's inner ring-road.
OPPOSITE PAGE Many of Dewsbury and Batley's wool warehouses have survived the shoddy cloth industry's changing fortunes.
The carved head of Benjamin Disraeli, as well as historical and mythical figures, now gaze down on a completely different world.

This decorative Dewsbury doorway of 1872, although semi-derelict a century later, survived to become the entrance to a disco.

DeVere House, originally built in 1871 for shipping agents Thornton, Homan & Co. to the designs of Lockwood and Mawson, is one of a number of export warehouses in the Little Germany area of Bradford. Most are decorated in the Italianate style then popular, creating a group of warehouse buildings unsurpassed in Britain.

THE WORLD
AT ITS FEET

From 1905 until 1975, passengers travelling by train through Lightcliffe near Halifax on the line between Bradford and Manchester, could glimpse a distinctive building proudly displaying the words BROOKES LIMITED in cut-out metal letters along the ridge of its roof.

This now demolished landmark was once the centre of a thriving quarrying and fireclay company founded in 1840 by Joseph Brooke. After his death in 1876 his sons continued to run and expand its operations, including a local mine and brickworks and quarries in Guernsey, Wales and Norway. Stone sets were also exported as far afield as South America.

Fireclay and glazed bricks in a variety of colours were produced, but the Company's reputation was built on a much used but little noticed product, 'Non-Slip Stone' flags, the basis of which was 'Silex', a hardwearing stone found eighty feet below the ground in the Lightcliffe area.

By 1910 upwards of 500 local authorities including The City of London, Birmingham, Newcastle, York and Leeds were regular customers. Even the promenades at Blackpool, Bridlington and other seaside towns were paved with 'Non-Slip Stone', as were railway station platforms throughout the country.

It seems incredible that a company making such a hugely successful product should fall into decline, but this happened in the 1960s. Plant and fixtures, including a railway system and steam locomotives were auctioned in 1969. The magnificent head office incorporating many of the company's products was demolished to make way for a washing machine factory.

ABOVE Joseph Brooke & Sons supplied glazed bricks for the construction of Bradford Exchange Station.
OPPOSITE PAGE TOP Brookes Limited head office at Lightcliffe near Halifax. Built in 1903 the building incorporated many of the company's stone based products.
OPPOSITE PAGE BOTTOM Brookes Limited.
BELOW Polishing stone at the Lightcliffe works of Brookes Limited.

ORIGINAL HOME BREW

Originally, most beer was brewed by publican brewers for consumption on their own premises, but by Victorian times there were breweries and malthouses in almost every town in the West Riding.

Richard Whitaker, the founder of one of the Yorkshire's most famous breweries, began as a publican brewer in Halifax. By 1848 he was running a small brewery in a group of cottages in Seedlings Mount, adjacent to the Stannary Inn, and a stone's throw from Halifax's North Bridge. Trade flourished as Whitaker's, like other breweries, bought up public houses and tied them to their own brands of beers.

The move to larger premises was completed when Seedlings Mount Brewery was built in 1860. Additional maltings and kilns were added in 1895, by which time the company had become Richard Whitaker and Sons Limited, Cock o' the North Brewery,

ABOVE Soothill Brewery on the outskirts of Batley. A change from beer to vinegar brewing failed to prevent its closure as a brewery in 1935. Used by a variety of industries thereafter, this relic of Yorkshire's once prolific brewing industry survived until the 1970s.
LEFT Hop presses in the mash room of Joshua Tetley & Son's Brewery, Leeds, 1880

Seedlings Mount Brewery, Halifax. Built in 1860 and famous for its Cock o' the North Ales. It survived a century of tribulation in the brewing industry to become one of the major brewers in Yorkshire, finally closing in 1969 following its take-over by Whitbreads. The building was demolished in 1973.

with an annual output of over fifty thousand barrels. This expansion ensured Whitakers survival at a time when many smaller breweries failed or were swallowed up by their more successful neighbours. Economic depression, and change in the licensing laws recommending a reduction in the number of outlets, made trading difficult for many breweries.

During the First World War the breweries traditional customers were away fighting for their country. Demand and production fell, raw materials were in short supply. A cottage industry only a century before, brewing had experienced the boom years but was, by the end of the First World War, dependent on the survival of the major players. Whitaker's became one of the four Halifax breweries to survive until the 1950s, its Cock o' the North brand name establishing a loyal following in Yorkshire and across the Pennines.

The final chapter of the Whitaker story was typical of the commercial climate of the 1960s, as take-overs began to re-model many of our industries. In 1969 the Whitaker family agreed to sell the company to Whitbread, one of the largest brewing chains in Britain. Closure came rapidly in the same year. Seedlings Mount Brewery stood derelict until demolition in 1973.

Heckmondwike, and Soothill Brewery near Batley were other earlier casualties. Heckmondwike Old Brewery Company Ltd., brewers and corn merchants, was established in 1860 by William Sykes, a solicitor, but ceased trading in 1901. Soothill Brewery in Grange Road had a slightly longer and more varied existence. Beer brewing ceased at Soothill during the First World War but was offered a new lease of life when in 1920 London vinegar brewers Grimble and Co. began vinegar production at Soothill, which continued until 1935, three years after being taken over by British Vinegars Ltd.

The tall main buildings of both breweries were typical of nineteenth century gravity fed breweries, where the crushed malt or grist is infused with hot water to make wort. At a lower level, hops are added and boiled in a copper before fermentation on the ground floor. Both buildings survived largely intact until their final demolition in the 1970s.

ABOVE Heckmondwike Old Brewery Company Ltd. Its chimney and tower dominated the town's skyline long after it ceased to be a brewery in 1901. RIGHT Decorative tiles and glasswork survive at the Garden Gate public house, once surrounded by shops and houses beside a busy main road in the Hunslet area of Leeds.

The entrance to Heckmondwike Old Brewery

FAREWELL STANLEY & CO

Look at an up-to-date large scale map of West Yorkshire, and among the contour lines and ring-roads you will find the words 'Dismantled Railway' appearing below a couple of finely ruled lines with a blank space between them. These blank, often disjointed ribbons meandering snake-like across the map, represent the topographical remnants of a once thriving railway system that spread like a web over this part of the county.

Without a doubt, the railways dramatically changed both the landscape and the lives of Victorian Britain. People and goods had never before travelled so fast or so far. Bricks made by the London Brick Company could be used to build a house on the outskirts of Wakefield, herring caught in the North Sea quickly found their way to the table of a Dewsbury mill-hand, whilst coal mined in Barnsley warmed terraced front-rooms in Bermondsey.

By the turn of the twentieth century the railway network was well established. Companies like the Lancashire & Yorkshire, Great Northern, Midland and the North Eastern had fought long and hard to capture the lucrative passenger and freight markets in Yorkshire's West Riding. Some even joined forces to share the spoils or outflank the opposition. Just about every town had a railway station. Some, like Heckmondwike, Brighouse and Birstall had two, with Dewsbury boasting three.

Here was a complete transport system which would seemingly last forever. For the first time, the people of the West Riding began to venture beyond the towns and villages in which they were born.

The expansion of commerce meant that clerks and managers 'commuted' to their city offices by train. Bradford mill-owners bought weekend retreats in Morecambe knowing that the 'Morecambe Residential' would deliver them to Forster Square Station and their board rooms by nine on a Monday morning.

ABOVE Built by the Great Northern Railway in 1874, Dewsbury Central
Station gave the town direct links with Bradford, Wakefield and London. The
Station closed in 1964 and the street-level entrance façade has been
incorporated into Dewsbury's inner-ring road.
RIGHT Passengers arriving at Dewsbury Central Station had upwards of thirty
steps to climb before reaching the platforms, hence the need for a porter.
OPPOSITE PAGE Stanley Station in about 1900. It was opened in 1865 and
was the only intermediate station on the five-mile long Methley Joint
Committee line between Lofthouse and Methley near Wakefield.

Stanley Station closed in 1964 and, like many buildings at the time, lay derelict until demolition in the 1970s. Apart from holiday excursion traffic, passenger services were mainly to Leeds, Wakefield and Castleford. Because Stanley was surrounded by the finest rhubarb growing land in the country, special rhubarb trains went from the town during the early spring.

The signal box at Gildersome West. With its stove and gas-lighting, signal boxes such as Gildersome offered an often solitary, self-contained existence of polished levers, dials and the 'tinging' of bells from the telegraph equipment. The line through Gildersome from Bradford to Wakefield via Morley closed in 1968.

ABOVE The Sutton twins, Morecambe 1950. Until the Beeching era, this Lancashire seaside resort could be reached from a number of local stations in the West Riding.

ABOVE Directions to the booking office survived the closure of Morley Top station in 1961.
RIGHT A Castleford to Cleethorpes excursion passing Lofthouse and Outwood in August 1964.

The railways also provided the means to escape the treadmill of work. Walking trips in the Yorkshire Dales via Skipton, Ilkley or Harrogate were regarded as a 'tonic' for town and city dwellers. But it was the annual holiday or day excursion to the coast that provided the real thrill of travelling by train.

The journey began from the 'up' or 'down' platforms of your local railway station. Stations like Stanley, the only one on the Methley Joint Railway between Lofthouse and Methley; Gildersome, on the line between Bradford, Morley and Wakefield; or Dewsbury Central on Bradford's other line to Wakefield via Batley.

A whistle from the guard and you were off. How long it took seemed irrelevant, nor did it matter that your coach was forty years old and on its last set of springs. There were no mills, mines, foundries or schools at the seaside. Out into open countryside rolled the train, with cows and sheep taking little notice of the billowing smoke. Past farms and woodland and swift running rivers. It all became part of the annual revival process, as the railways ingrained themselves into the fabric of our lives.

Now where passengers once stood on the platforms of Stanley, Gildersome and Dewsbury Central, people watch television in their living rooms, drive forklift trucks or speed round a busy inner ring-road. Three stations, which, like many others, departed forever on a single ticket issued by a certain Dr. Beeching.

THE END OF THE LINE

The origins of Bradford Exchange Station go back to 1850, when the Lancashire & Yorkshire Railway opened Bradford's second railway station, Drake Street. The first was Market Street (later renamed Forster Square) built in 1846 by the Leeds & Bradford Railway Company and the terminus of the city's first railway link with Leeds.

Drake Street Station gave Yorkshire's fast-growing wool city a link via the Spen and Calder valleys to Lancashire, and in particular to the capital of the cotton industries, Manchester. In an era of intense railway building activity, Bradford acquired its third railway station in 1854. The grandly named Leeds, Bradford and Halifax Junction Railway brought in a second line from Leeds Central Station to its own terminus, which was some distance away from the city centre at Adolphus Street. This piecemeal approach to railway building often had its drawbacks. Because it was on a hill on Bradford's southern slopes, the new station was never popular. However, it did allow its passengers to travel to London from Bradford, albeit in a journey of over five hours.

In 1867 its passenger trains, by this time run by the Great Northern Railway, were transferred to the Lancashire & Yorkshire's Drake Street Station, which by then had become known as Bradford Exchange, and where an extra platform had been added. What must have seemed like a sound idea at the time turned out to be a disaster. Trains moving in and out of Exchange Station had to squeeze through a double track tunnel that ran beneath a densely populated area of the city, creating a smoky, sulphurous bottleneck made even worse by the

Horse-drawn cabs were once a common sight at stations like Bradford Exchange. This wooden cab-man's shelter survived until the stations closure, before finding a new home at the National Tramway Museum, Crich, Derbyshire.

ABOVE LEFT Sunlight plays upon the decorative spandrels supporting the twin 100 feet spans of Bradford Exchange Station.

ABOVE The days of steam powered holiday excursions from Bradford Exchange are drawing to a close in August 1967.

LEFT A section of the fine panelled mural wall that ran almost the whole length of Bradford Exchange Station façade facing the Victoria Hotel.

additional Great Northern trains. The railway companies and their passengers soon grew impatient. In 1876 houses and streets were swept aside to enable the tunnel to be opened up into a wide cutting with extra tracks, providing a prelude to the complete rebuilding of Exchange Station and creating one of Bradford's most memorable landmarks.

It is perhaps worth mentioning that even today many railway 'buffs' believe that an opportunity to build a new Bradford Central station serving the Midland, Great Northern and Lancashire & Yorkshire railway companies was missed. Had it been built, it would have put Bradford on a through main line from the south to Scotland via Carlisle. But the idea was rejected by all the companies involved. For some, Bradford's unlinked twin stations would forever relegate the city's railway status to nothing more than a couple of branch line termini. Branch line or not, the new Bradford Exchange rose from the rubble of the old and was opened in 1888.

Passengers approaching the station could have been forgiven for feeling somewhat disappointed by its main entrance. There were no impressive columns and pediment as at London's Euston Station, or the arched central portico of Newcastle Central. A simple doorway and a flight of steps took you from street level to the station itself. Only when you reached the top of these rather gloomy stairs did Bradford Exchange Station become all that a railway terminus should.

The stations ten platforms were covered by two magnificent semi-circular glazed arches, each spanning a hundred feet and supported in the centre by eighteen Corinthian cast-iron columns and wrought-iron spandrels with decorative scrollwork made by Thornton and Crebbin at their nearby Hammerton Street foundry. On what could have been a blank wall facing the Victoria Hotel, the architect seized the opportunity to create a masterpiece of mural architecture running almost the full length of the building.

Most of the stations finest hours were shared with the age of steam. The Great Northern, in its green livery, later the LNER, running alongside the black of the Lancashire & Yorkshire, later the LMS. Ornate wooden-bodied bogie coaches with gas lighting, horse-drawn hansom cabs, enamel signs and posters advertising excursions and Bank Holiday specials.

At a local level, frequent train services connected Bradford with Leeds, Wakefield, Huddersfield, Halifax and Keighley.

ABOVE 'The South Yorkshireman' leaving Bradford Exchange for London, Marylebone, photographed by Leslie Overend in 1948.
OPPOSITE PAGE Deserted, and devoid of most of its glazing, the station still retains an air of quiet dignity shortly before closure in 1973. The demolition that followed uncovered a 1920s poster advertising Preston Dock as the 'port for East Lancashire and West Yorkshire'.

There were trains to Manchester and Liverpool and summer specials to the coast and resorts of Southport, Cleethorpes and Skegness. For those with deeper pockets, Bradford had its share of prestigious named trains. 'The Yorkshire Pullman', 'The White Rose', 'The West Riding' and 'The South Yorkshireman' enabled the wealthy to travel to London in style.

The last steam train left Bradford Exchange on October 1st 1967. By the 1970s the station began to mirror the neglect to be found in Kirkgate Market, less than half-a-mile away. The early days of the railways were fiercely competitive, but no one could have foreseen the strength of competition from road transport.

Even as the demolition gangs' acetylene torches began to disfigure and dismember the station's decorative ironwork, work had begun on a transport interchange close by, where, in a rare spirit of co-operation, buses and trains would exist side by side, thus reviving the fortunes of public transport. In the process Bradford Exchange Station was totally obliterated. Its sheer size and splendour gave the railway a presence in the city. Something conspicuously absent in its hybrid four-platform successor.

Eighty-five years after being made in a Bradford iron foundry, these wrought iron
spandrels from Bradford Exchange Station ended up a tangled web of scrap.

The dismembered wrought-iron spine that once held aloft the ribs supporting Bradford Exchange's magnificent twin-arched roofs await the cutter's torch.

SEND IT BY ROAD

The site of Cleckheaton railway station and goods yard is now occupied by a car park and supermarket, its shelves stacked with hundreds of products which in the past would have been bought from a dozen or more separate shops.

This seven-day-a-week mecca of one-stop shopping is kept topped up by giant articulated lorries moving between depots and the company's stores via the motorway network, the first eight miles of which opened in 1958 as the Preston bypass. This, along with the M1 opened in 1959, represented the dawn of Britain's road transport revolution and the beginning of the end for hundreds of local railway stations and goods yards.

Until the 1960's, the railway goods yard was vital to the prosperity of the area it served. They were a part of the urban landscape, and apart from the clanking of buffers and couplings as wagons were shunted around, few gave them a second glance. Just about every bicycle, tractor, tin of peas, piano, fillet of fish and lump of coal arrived on our doorsteps by rail, as did the raw

A Huddersfield to Bradford train passes through the busy goods yard at Cleckheaton Central Station in the late 1950s. The site is now occupied by a supermarket.

When first built, the Great Northern and Lancashire & Yorkshire Railway companies shared North Bridge goods warehouse, Halifax.
The town's wide manufacturing base meant that an extraordinary variety of products passed through its loading bays.
It was closed in 1964, and lay derelict for a further ten years before being demolished.

materials for our manufacturing industries which, in turn, were ultimately sent on their way from the nearest goods yard.

Railway tracks disappeared into sheds equipped with loading platforms, weighing scales and cranes. To one side, was an office where clerks recorded every consignment – its origin, size, weight and eventual destination.

Outside the sheds, overhead lamps, loading gauges, signals, carts and a variety of railway vans and trucks combined to make up a typical local goods yard, a scene which inevitably included a siding around which clustered a row of coal bunkers, weighing machines, and a handful of scruffy wooden sheds from where the local coal merchants operated.

Much grander were the yards at the major railway centres of Leeds, Bradford, Wakefield, Halifax, Huddersfield and Dewsbury, where magnificent warehouses were built to hold vast quantities of merchandise, including wool, grain, tea and a host of other commodities. The railway sidings here covered several acres and were part of an operation that worked round the clock.

Railway goods' yards could be dangerous places. The continual movement of railway engines, trucks, lorries and horses, were all potential hazards, forcing the railway companies to display warning signs. Like everything else in the railway vernacular, these signs were made to last. Written in the terminology of years gone by, they were still proclaiming their messages long after the last goods train had snaked out of the sidings and the wrecking ball began the destruction of another unsung monument to the past.

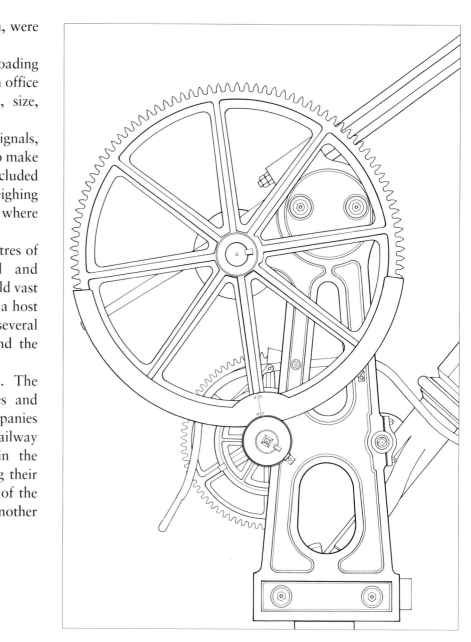

This nineteenth century hand-operated 5 ton crane was used in the goods yard at Mirfield until the 1960s, and was typical of much of the equipment that survived until the end of the local railway goods yard era.

The importance of the railways as the prime mover of goods meant that Earlsheaton, a small village barely a mile from the centre of Dewsbury, had its own goods yard and shed. Built by the Great Northern Railway, it covered a single track using three hand-operated cranes. The line through Earlsheaton closed in 1964, leaving the goods shed to fall derelict before final demolition ten years later.

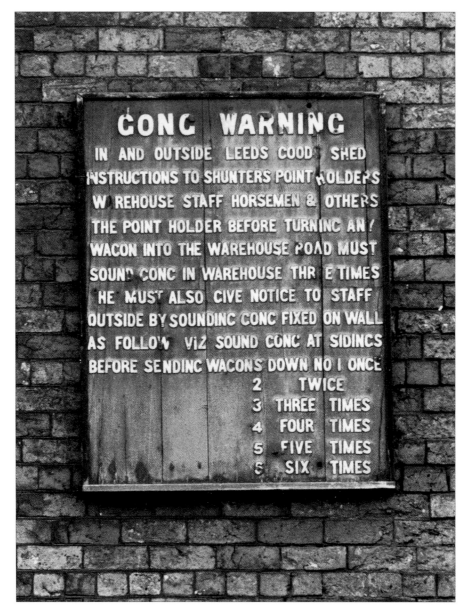

GONG WARNING
IN AND OUTSIDE LEEDS GOODS SHED
INSTRUCTIONS TO SHUNTERS POINT HOLDERS
WAREHOUSE STAFF HORSEMEN & OTHERS
THE POINT HOLDER BEFORE TURNING ANY
WAGON INTO THE WAREHOUSE ROAD MUST
SOUND GONG IN WAREHOUSE THREE TIMES
HE MUST ALSO GIVE NOTICE TO STAFF
OUTSIDE BY SOUNDING GONG FIXED ON WALL
AS FOLLOW VIZ SOUND GONG AT SIDINGS
BEFORE SENDING WAGONS DOWN NO I ONCE
2   TWICE
3   THREE TIMES
4   FOUR TIMES
5   FIVE TIMES
6   SIX . TIMES

ABOVE Warning signs like this, in the now demolished Wellington Street goods yard,
Leeds, were a constant reminder of the dangers facing railway employees.
OPPOSITE PAGE Leeds Central Station's goods yards were on two different levels.
To transfer wagons from the low level Great Northern Railway yard to the Lancashire
& Yorkshire Railway's warehouse a steam-powered hoist capable of lifting twenty tons
was built. Its monumental shell has survived to become a feature in a retail park.

GENTLEMEN

By the end of the nineteenth century electric trams were becoming a common sight. For a few pence you could travel to work and back. If not, and the longer the walk, the more likely you were to get 'caught short'. These humble stone and brick 'conveniences', and many others like them, must have witnessed many a last minute dash on a cold winter's morning.

It's a man's world. Castleford, heartland of Rugby League football, 1973.

A Victorian open-top gas-lit 'convenience', John William Street, Huddersfield.

Influences from Art Deco cinema architecture bring a touch of style to this 'gents' in Churwell Hill, Leeds.

GINNELS & SNICKETS

The use of the word 'ginnel' to describe a narrow alleyway is thought to be uniquely West Riding. 'Snicket' or 'nicket' are probably even more local, but their origins are now lost.

The almost organic way in which our urban landscape evolved resulted in the creation of a myriad of narrow passage ways. Some date to the 1870s when bye-laws were passed compelling builders of back-to back houses to provide passage ways giving access to shared yards, outside toilets and ash pits. In the days when most people moved around locally on foot, building up a personal knowledge of their surroundings, the whereabouts of these hidden alleyways would provide welcome short-cuts from home to work, shops, school or railway station. The words 'ginnel' and 'snicket' unique in themselves, reflect this local knowledge, but bring a quizzical expression to those who know nothing of their meaning.

A long walk was saved by a short but formidable looking tunnel underneath the Leeds – Manchester railway line at Batley Carr near Dewsbury.

A distinctively proportioned narrow doorway led to the rear yard of a row of back-to-back houses in Wortley Leeds.

Ginnels or snickets? Square lintel and stone arch in Low Moor, Bradford, typify the idiosyncratic nature of some nineteenth century house building.

A decorative date-stone marks the entrance to a passageway between two houses at Mountain near Queensbury.

Four shapely iron bollards and a short length of steel girder guard the entrance to an overgrown alleyway off Gelderd Road, Armley, Leeds.

BRUSH STROKES IN RETREAT

Most passers-by pay scant attention to the sign painted on the gable end of a row of houses in Birstall, near Batley, advertising a long gone flock manufacturer. Another sign in Heckmondwike offers tea at 1d a cup. And what were 'Grandrilles' and 'Satteens' lettered on the doorway of the former Wm. Sugden & Sons premises in Cleckheaton?

These simple fading messages, through their styles of lettering and the products they advertise, give us a glimpse of the times in which they were first painted. Images of our towns and cities from the early days of photography show a wealth of painted signs on shops, theatres, public houses and railway stations, with a richness of style and a variety of letterforms – some based on letterpress printed ephemera – the like of which we shall probably never see again.

Sign-writers, many starting their working lives as painters and decorators, learned their skills through apprenticeships. Traditional sign-writing still continues, but the use of plastics and computer guided laser-cutting technology has largely turned sign-writing into sign-making better able to respond commercially to the needs and language of our times.

ABOVE 'Tea at 1d and 1½d a cup'. Market Street, Heckmondwike.
LEFT Years of weathering have revealed that this painted sign on a piece of slate began life in Manor Row in the centre of Bradford, before being turned upside down and over-painted with the numbers of a group of cottages in Low Moor on the outskirts of the city.

ABOVE 'Side-curtains and Motor Hoods'. From the early days of motoring.
Seen in a yard off Briggate, Leeds, in 1973.
RIGHT A slowly fading reminder of one of Cleckheaton's many textile related
industries.

LEFT Once resplendent in gold and reminiscent of the
familiar Hovis and Turog Bread signs, the cut-out wooden
letters of this example in Northgate, Halifax, offered a
more permanent variation in painted signs.

OPPOSITE PAGE A painted sign familiar to travellers on the
A62 between Leeds and Huddersfield that has long outlived
the mill it advertises.

ON THE LEVEL

From the outset, our pioneer railway builders accepted the basic premise that, whatever the lie of the land, railway lines should be as level as possible. This principle was even more relevant half a century earlier to the surveyors and engineers of our canals, to whom level really did mean *level*. Valleys were crossed by embankments and aqueducts, and hills subjugated by flights of locks and tunnels.

This 'needs must' approach to building must have been an inspiration to the early nineteenth century visionaries hoping to link our growing centres of industry and commerce with iron rails and steam power. No matter how steep, hills and valleys would present no problem. The West Riding of Yorkshire is well endowed with both. Consequently, we enjoy a rich, and in some cases spectacular collection of embankments, cuttings, tunnels and bridges.

The Great Northern Railway for instance, went to great lengths – and heights – to bring a railway to the more remote parts of the West Riding. On the moors above Bradford and Halifax, on a line connecting them with Keighley, stands Hewenden Viaduct. Built in 1884, it crosses the valley below Manywells Reservoir in a bold but gentle curve. Peering down from a carriage window at Hewenden Beck 123 feet below must have been the nearest sensation to flying for many passengers travelling on the line. The last passenger train rumbled over Hewenden Viaduct in May 1955 but its presence in the landscape remains undiminished.

There could be no greater contrast to this monumental structure than a wooden footbridge which, until the mid-1960s straddled the Roundwood colliery branch line on the outskirts of Wakefield. This gravity defying creation of indeterminate age and origin belonged to the allotment-garden school of architecture. Plans and blueprints appeared to have been ignored in favour of a quick sketch on a scrap of paper. No two pieces of timber seemed to be the same in length or thickness, but the end result was not without a certain rugged gracefulness and it had a quirky empathy with its immediate landscape, surrounded by hawthorn, brambles and the roughly laid colliery railway track.

Most of our great bridges and viaducts were built in stone, with fine examples still to be found at Thornton, Lockwood, and Kirkstall. A mile long viaduct said to contain 800,000,000 bricks brings the railway from Doncaster into Wakefield.

Travellers journeying from Wakefield to Halifax by road entered the town by crossing Hebble Brook at the foot of Beacon Hill. A substantial six-arch stone viaduct built in 1772 was replaced by the present iron bridge of 1871 by John Fraser.

The twin spans of Halifax's North Bridge would grace the approach to just about any town in Britain. Although well cared for, since 1973 it has been overpowered by a pre-stressed concrete high-level road bridge, which already has needed a costly major rebuilding program: an indignity never suffered during the long life of the elegant ancestor in its shadow.

ABOVE A Great Northern Railway tank engine and its teak bodied coaches are dwarfed by the monumental scale of
Hewenden Viaduct on the now closed lines between Bradford, Halifax and Keighley. Today it's seventeen arches still provide
a dramatic contrast to it's wild moorland setting.
OPPOSITE PAGE Built originally by the West Riding & Grimsby Railway in 1866, the mile long Wakefield viaduct carries the
Doncaster-Leeds main line into Wakefield Westgate Station on ninety-five brick arches.

North Bridge, Halifax, built in 1871, spans Hebble Brook and the rubble of progress during the construction of the Hebble Viaduct in 1973. The modern photograph shows how the concrete viaduct completely dwarfs it's elegant Victorian predecessor.

BELOW A bridge built in 1878 at Savile Town, Dewsbury, still crosses the short branch canal linking the Dewsbury basin with the main Aire and Calder Navigation.

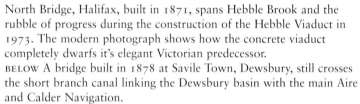

In rustic harmony with its surroundings; a wooden footbridge over a branch line connecting Roundwood Colliery with the Wakefield, Bradford railway line. Although surviving until the mid-1960s, both railway line and bridge have now completely disappeared from the landscape.

SERMON
ON THE
MOUNT

In 1742, three years after founding the Methodist church in Bristol with his brother Charles, John Wesley rode north to Newcastle-on-Tyne. Over the next forty years Wesley covered tens of thousands of miles in his quest to spread the gospel through the ministry of Methodism.

Waiting to offer him hospitality on his journey north was a Birstall stonemason, John Nelson, who had become an early convert to the movement after attending one of Wesley's meetings in London. Nelson himself later came to be regarded as a pioneer of Methodism in Yorkshire, persuading Wesley to hold two of his famous open-air meetings on Birstall Hill and Dewsbury Moor.

The seeds of Methodism in West Yorkshire had been sown. The harvest would yield the swelling congregations of Wesleyan Methodists, Primitive Methodists, Independent Methodists, Baptists, and Congregationalists; whilst their chapels and meeting houses became a feature of every town.

Wesley's evangelical spirit and tireless energy took him to even more remote pastures. In 1747 he preached in the open-air at Heptonstall on the moors high above the Calder Valley. An area that would, only twenty years later, become the setting for a quite different social drama, the story of the Cragg Vale Coiners, a group of men who fell foul of the law by shearing clippings from gold guineas, melting them down and re-casting them as new coins. The plot not only involved forgery but murder, and in 1770 their leader 'King' David Hartley was hanged at Tyburn near York.

Wesley returned to Heptonstall in 1764 to open the Methodist Chapel. Originally octagonal in plan, but extended in 1802, it survives as the oldest Methodist chapel still in regular use in the

ABOVE Heptonstall Methodist Chapel, built in 1764 and regularly visited by the founders of Methodism John and Charles Wesley, and now the oldest in the world in continuous use.
OPPOSITE PAGE A flight of eighteen steps had to be climbed by worshippers at Bethesda Primitive Methodist Chapel, perched on the edge of Beacon Hill at Southowram above Halifax.

world. Over the next century many small communities in the Pennines built chapels or meeting houses. Like John Wesley himself, slight of build but robust in character, these chapels with their unadorned symmetry have few pretensions or attempt to up-stage the magnificence of their moorland surroundings. Inside, there is the same restraint. Polished pews and brass-work glow, lit by windows with simple stained-glass borders. A clock on the rear wall facing the pulpit serves as a gentle reminder of time's passing.

If this was Nonconformity expressed in its humblest form, something much less modest could be found in some West Riding towns. Upper Independent Chapel in Heckmondwike was built in 1890 and could seat a congregation of over a thousand, attracting eminent preachers from far and wide. With its Corinthian columns and pediment it resembled an imposing town hall. The interior was equally impressive, with a carved oak pulpit, carpeted pews and spacious gallery.

The local worthies and ordinary folk who, on a wave of confidence and self-assurance, raised £11,264.7s.3d. to build what was the last of five huge chapels in the Spen Valley, would be dismayed at the sight of Upper Independent Chapel today. Having held its last service in 1977, Heckmondwike's most notable building now wears the haunted look of terminal decline.

Most of the large town chapels have either been demolished, or now serve a different purpose. In many ways their isolation from the relentless march of progress has meant that many moorland chapels have survived. Cragg Vale's purposeful architecture and simple plan have readily translated into a distinctive family home in a superb setting. The waves created by John Wesley's visits to the Pennine foothills over two and a half centuries ago may now be just a ripple. But Heptonstall, Blackshawhead and others continue to minister to the spiritual needs of the communities they serve.

LEFT Blackshawhead Wesleyan Chapel, built in 1815 and enlarged in 1899, continues to serve this small moorland community between Hebden Bridge and Todmorden.

BELOW Symmetry and simplicity are the key architectural virtues found in most Calder Valley chapels, as here at Blackshawhead. Decorative glass window borders add the minimum of exterior decoration, but viewed from the inside, with sunlight streaming through, the combination of rich reds and blues is nothing short of stunning.

BELOW LEFT No greater contrast could be found to these moorland chapels than the now fading grandeur of Upper Independent Chapel, Heckmondwike. Built in 1890 when Nonconformity in the mill towns of the West Riding was at it's height.

The warm welcoming glow from the polished woodwork inside Blackshawhead is in sharp contrast to the chapel's unpretentious exterior.

ABOVE Storm clouds form a dramatic backdrop to Flockton Zion United Reformed Chapel, built in 1802 on high ground between Huddersfield and Wakefield.

OPPOSITE PAGE Cragg Vale is a picturesque wooded valley that eventually cradles Cragg Brook on its way from its source near Blackstone Edge Moor to Mytholmroyd on the River Calder. This magnificent setting has probably been the salvation of Cragg Vale Methodist Chapel. Closed in the 1970s and facing dereliction, it was eventually saved from destruction and is now a private house.

THE FINAL REEL

In the autumn of 1888 a small group assembled at the house of French photographer Louis Aime Augustin Le Prince, in Woodhouse Lane, Leeds, to witness the world's first 'animated picture' show, a short film taken with Le Prince's own camera showing pedestrians and horse drawn vehicles crossing Leeds Bridge.

This important but little known milestone in cinematic history pre-dates similar demonstrations by Thomas Alva Edison and his Kinetoscope in New York in 1894, and the Lumiere Brothers, Cinematographe in 1895, who gave their first demonstration to a paying audience in London the following year.

Moving photographic images must have been nothing short of sensational to those early audiences, even though the running time of each film was only a few minutes. Titles and subjects featured were to say the least fairly prosaic. *The Blacksmith at Work, Babies Playing, Cavalry Horses being Watered,* and *The Arrival of a Train at Coitat Station.* An audience in Huddersfield it seems, rushed for the exits when they saw the train approaching!

The power of the moving image began to match the pull of the live variety theatre. Town Halls, Temperance Halls and skating rinks doubled-up as cinemas in these early days. As cinema audiences grew these semi-permanent halls became unsuitable, leading to the establishment of Britain's first true cinemas, the 'Electric Palaces'.

The use of the word 'electric' sounds more advanced than it really was, for at this stage in the second decade of the twentieth century films were devoid of sound tracks. Instead, they were dependent for their accompaniment on the cinema pianist, whose concentration on the 'action' would be sorely tested by the cheering, jeering, whistling, foot-stamping audiences of the West Riding. Quite a few cinema pianists must have breathed a

'In a Den of Lions' promises an exciting time for patrons, and a busy evening for the pianist accompanying the short films included in the Variety bill at the Royal Electric Theatre, Hebden Bridge, photographed in 1913

sigh of relief when the 'talkies' arrived in the late 1920s.

By then the cinema was so popular that many towns had more than one 'Electric Palace'. In a world where the radio was the only form of mass entertainment, sound and colour took film making to even greater heights of fantasy, glamour and style, epitomised in the new era of 'super cinemas'. The New Victoria, Bradford (later renamed the Gaumont) seated over three thousand people and included a café and ballroom.

It is ironic to think that during this 'Golden Era' of the

cinema, John Logie Baird was working on an invention that would eventually contribute to the death of nearly every 'Electric Palace' in the West Riding. With the advent of television, the 'flea-pit' down town, which probably hadn't had a coat of paint in years, began to look rather drab and uninviting. Then Bingo! a craze in the sixties and seventies brought a brief respite. The world of the 'movies' has now gone 'Multiplex', but some 'Electric Palaces' still survive – as discount carpet warehouses, tyre fitting companies, or as in one instance, a mosque.

RIGHT The construction of a dual-carriageway narrowly missed this classic 'Electric Palace'. The Picture Palace, Dudley Hill, on the outskirts of Bradford, built in 1912 during the era of the 'golden silents', eventually became the first cinema in Bradford to be fitted with central heating. After closure in 1967, it followed many of it's contemporaries by becoming a Bingo hall.

BELOW Honley's cinema opened in 1914 as the Picture Palace, before a change of name at the end of the First World War to the Palladium. One of the early casualties to television, the cinema closed in 1961, lying derelict for almost a decade before it's conversion to a leisure centre.

ABOVE Audiences reached their peak in the 1930s with the opening of 'super' cinemas like the New Victoria, Bradford; the third largest cinema in Great Britain at the time.

LEFT The Electric Theatre, tucked away in the back streets of Marsden at the head of the Colne Valley ten miles from Huddersfield. Opened in 1919 it had a seating capacity for 550. In the early 1930s the R.C.A. 'Photophone' sound-on-film system was installed. The Electric Theatre was run by one of Yorkshire's early film pioneers Tom Leyland, who toured fairgrounds with his Electric Pictures. His family continued to run the cinema until the death of his daughter, Mrs. Laura Beardsall in 1975. The cinema was demolished in 1979.

FURTHER READING

Ayers, John, *Architecture in Bradford* (Whatmoughs Limited, on behalf of the Bradford Civic Society), 1973

Allen, Eleanor, *Wash and Brush Up* (Adam & Charles Black, London), 1976

Barber, N., *A Century of British Brewers, 1890-1990* (The Brewery History Society), 1990

Bodey, Hugh, *Textiles, Past-into-Present Series* (B.T. Batsford Ltd.), 1976

Bradford Libraries and Information Service, *Textile Voices: Mill Life this Century*, 1989

Bentley, Phyllis, Dr., *The Pennine Weaver* (Firecrest Publishing Limited), 1971

Bairstow, Martin, *The Great Northern Railway in West Yorkshire* (M. Bairstow), 1982

Bairstow, Martin, *The Manchester & Leeds Railway, The Calder Valley Line* (M. Bairstow), 1987

Chapman, Stephen, & Rose, Peter, *Railway Memories No6 Ardsley, Wakefield & Normanton* (Bellcode Books), 1994

Caffyn, Lucy, *Workers Housing in West Yorkshire 1750-1920* (RCHME & HMSO), 1986

Capon, John, *John & Charles Wesley, The Preacher and the Poet* (Hodder and Stoughton), 1988

Ellis, Norman, *West Yorkshire Railway Stations* (Bond Publications) 1988

Giles, Colum, & Goodhall, Ian, H., *Yorkshire Textile Mills 1770-1930* (HMSO London), 1992

Godfrey, Alan, *Old Ordnance Survey Maps of North & West Yorkshire*

Huddersfield Geology Group, *Rocks and Landscapes of Huddersfield*, 1998

Hammond, Martin, *Bricks and Brickmaking*,(Shire Publications Ltd.), 1981

Haigh, H., Malcolm, *The History of Batley 1800-1974* (Malcolm H. Haigh), 1978

Hird, Douglas, *History of the Spen Valley 1780s-1980s* (Douglas Hird), 1985

Jenkins, D. T., & Ponting K. G. *The British Wool Textile Industry 1770-1914* (Heinemann Educational Books Ltd.), 1982

Lackey, Clifford, *Quality Pays... The Story of Joshua Tetley & Son* (Springwood Books Limited), 1985

Lewry, A. J., *Sign Written Art* (David & Charles), 1989

Lindley, Kenneth, *Chapels and Meeting Houses* (John Baker Publishing Ltd.),1969

Linstrum, Derek, *West Yorkshire Architects and Architecture* (Lund Humphries), 1978

Marsh, John, *Clip a Bright Guinea, The Yorkshire Coiners of the 18th Century* (Smith Settle)

Mellor, C.J., *Picture Pioneers, The Story of the Northern Cinema 1896-1971* (Franck Graham), 1971

Newberry, Maggie, *Picking up Threads. Reminiscences of a Bradford Mill Girl* (Bradford Libraries), 1993

Priestley, J.B., *The World of J.B. Priestley* (Hienemann London), 1967

Smithies, Philip, *The Architecture of the Halifax Piece Hall 1775-1779* (C.P. Smithies) 1988

Sheeran, George, *Railway Buildings of West Yorkshire 1812-1920* (Ryburn Publishing), 1994

Smith, Stuart, R. & Hornsey, Brian, *The Cinemas of Huddersfield and Surrounding Area (Kirklees)* (Mercia Cinema Society), 2000

Singleton, Fred, *Industrial Revolution in Yorkshire* (Dalesman), 1970

Thornes, R.C.N. *West Yorkshire, 'A Noble Scene of Industry' The Development of the County, 1500-1830* (West Yorkshire County Council), 1981

Varo, Stanley, *A Mercantile Meander* (Stanley Varo) 1989

Vallings, Sylvia, & Wood Lesley, *A Photographer's Dewsbury Shops & Shopping* (Kirklees Libraries, Museums and Arts Division)

Wild, Jack, & Chapman, Stephen, *Railway Memories No11 Halifax & the Calder Valley* (Bellcode Books), 1998